Film Actresses

Volume 23

Dolores del Rio

Documentary study

Part 1

ISBN-13 : 978-1502987686

ISBN-10 : 1502987686

Dtp
and
graphic design

Iacob Adrian

Author statement

The actors and actresses are the the bricks .

The cast and crew are the plaster .

They stand on the foundation created by
producers and writers and directors .

All these people creates the great palace
of the art of film .

Iacob Adrian - 2013

Dolores Del Rio reveals her
secrets of marital happiness

by VAL LEWTON

*Author of "No Bed of Her Own,"
"Yearly Lease" and "Head of the
House"*

How to
Hold a
Husband
In Hollywood

"SEPARATION IS VERY bad, especially in Hollywood. It's dangerous to leave your husband or your wife alone in Hollywood. There are too many temptations; too many charming, handsome and interesting people," says Dolores Del Rio, and when she says it her great, dark eyes, that seem to have two stars of light fixed in their depths, grow very large and very serious.

For marriage to Dolores Del Rio, who has been married twice, once miserably and, the second time happily, is a very serious thing.

Interviewed in her suite at the Hotel Sherry-Netherlands on a recent visit to New York with her husband, Cedric Gibbons, a Hollywood art director, Dolores tried to give her recipe for marital happiness when the conversation veered—as it always does—to Hollywood marriages, their success and their failure. Charming in a frock of dull black silk, with collars and cuffs of pleated white crêpe, and wearing a bracelet of emerald beads on her left wrist and two matched rings of square cut emerald on either hand, she spoke frankly and yet with a certain, almost childish dignity.

Dolores Del Rio is one of the few picture stars who is actually more beautiful in life than she is on the screen. I had gone to see her in the expectation of the more mature beauty one sees in her film plays. I was unprepared for her almost girlish charm. She is very young and off the screen she looks so. Seeing her as portrayed by the camera

one can form no conception of how lovely is the texture of her dark complexion, the brilliant smoothness of her cheeks, and the glossiness of her black hair. But it takes, I realize, more than mere beauty to hold an interesting husband for more than three years in the emotional maelstrom of Hollywood. And what it takes, Dolores Del Rio has in large abundance.

● When I questioned her about her happiness in marriage and contrasted it with the dismaying flood of divorces that poured out of Hollywood this year, she smiled.

"You must know," she said, "that my friends were all saying when I married Cedric that it would only last two or three weeks. They even told me that, and they told it to Cedric. But we thought we knew better, and you see we did!"

She raised expressive hands in a gay gesture as she said this, then went on:

"It's been frightful, hasn't it, the number of divorces and separations this year?"

I listed the most important of them for her benefit: Doug and Mary; Doug, Jr., and Joan; Carole Lombard and Bill Powell; Adrienne Ames and her broker husband; Lew Ayres and Lola Lane; Ann Harding and Harry Bannister. Dolores' expressive eyes registered dismay.

"Too many divorces for so small a town," she said. "But

How to Hold a Husband in Hollywood

then you mustn't forget that Hollywood is a hard place to be happy unless you're so absorbed in your work that you haven't time to get into mischief. I do believe what I say when I tell you that no married person should leave husband or wife alone in Hollywood. There's too much temptation. Think of all the charming, intelligent people out there."

It seemed a fresh viewpoint, but it reminded me of a theory of Donald Henderson Clarke, author of *Millie* and other popular novels. In one of his books he remarked that fidelity is a matter of association, that absence may make the heart grow fonder, but usually for someone else, in a paraphrase of the song.

DOLORES HAD MET Clarke in Hollywood when he was writing the original story for her next picture, *Dance of Desire*. She spoke of what an engaging man he is and how much she had enjoyed meeting him.

"He knows much about the world," she said. "I like men like that."

This reminded her of further details in her present domestic happiness.

"It's one reason Cedric and I get along so well. We like the same people. Our friends are usually writers, directors or artists; people who think."

I ventured the remark that this seemed a knock at her own profession. She was quick to deny it.

"Oh, don't misunderstand me. I like actors and I like actresses. We've lots of them among our friends. But I like writers and artists and directors better; they're more creative. Cedric feels the same way about it. But then we feel so much the same way about so many things; even sports. We both like tennis and swimming and dislike horseback riding and golf.

"I think," she said, suddenly thoughtful, "that that's the best foundation for marriage; liking the same things. You can't imagine how I appreciate being married to a man in the picture business. He can understand why it is that I sometimes have to miss dinner at home and work half the night at the studio, and he can listen intelligently when I tell him about the day's work, and what he has to say—because he is in the same business—is interesting and vital to me."

She paused for a moment to jump up and peep into the bedroom of her hotel suite, where her husband was impatiently waiting for the interview to be concluded. After three and a half years, a husband who frets and fumes at every minute spent away from his wife is certainly in love with her. Assured that her husband was peaceful and happy in the bedroom, Dolores returned and went on:

"You know, I really think," she said, "that one of the greatest lures of Hollywood is work and at the same time one of the greatest curses. Now Cedric and I are happy because we're both immersed in our work; we live and talk pictures day after day. Not that we don't like amusements, plays and books and parties and dancing. We do these things together, but we work alone. That keeps us from getting into one of those married mental ruts. Every time we see each other we have fresh ideas to contribute, studio news to exchange and by the end

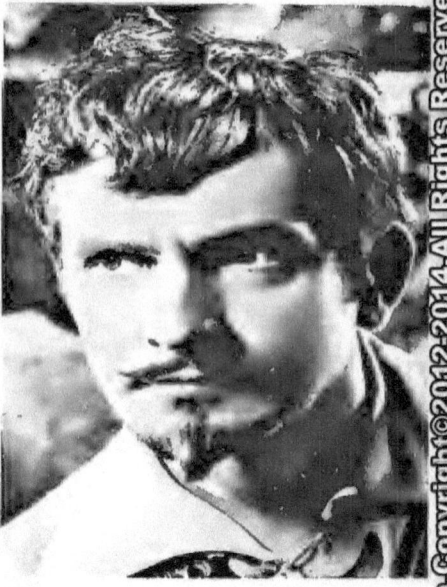

Of course you remember this gentleman! Come, come; it's Fredric March in character for The Firebrand, *romance of the 16th Century in which he is appearing with Constance Bennett*

of the day we're both tired enough to enjoy our home."

I had heard about Dolores Del Rio's home. Designed by her artist husband in the most recent of the modern trends, this home is one of the seven wonders of Hollywood. I asked about it.

"Our home is lovely!" the star exclaimed. "It's been built just for our own needs and our own ideas of comfort; that's what makes it so perfect and beautiful."

I told her I had seen pictures of her home in a magazine.

"Oh, I'm glad! I'm so proud of our house," she exclaimed. "And of my dog! Did you ever see pictures of my dog?"

But I had never seen pictures of her dog.

"He's a bull terrier—a lovely white dog. We call him Michael. Both of us love him. We're going to mate him this year and have puppies."

I asked her if this dog really occupied a miniature replica of her bed and is served at her table just like a human being as has been reported.

"Oh, yes, I do have a little bed for him just like my own and he does sleep in my room—but he eats in the kitchen," she said.

When I prepared to leave Dolores smiled and said,

"The only thing you haven't asked me is what I eat. Isn't that part of the repertory of interviewers?"

"Well, what do you eat?"

"Everything—and look—" she pressed slim brown hands against her precise hips, "—I don't even have to worry about diet."

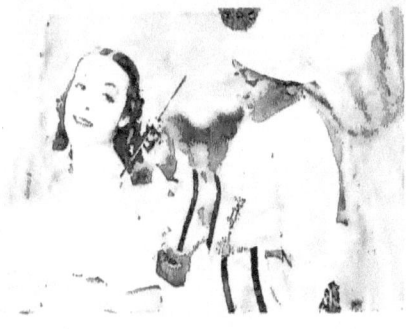

Dolores Del Rio enjoys the services of her official backscratcher in an amusing scene

Madame Du Barry

HOLDS COURT

ADVANCE SCENES FROM DOLORES DEL RIO'S NEW PICTURE

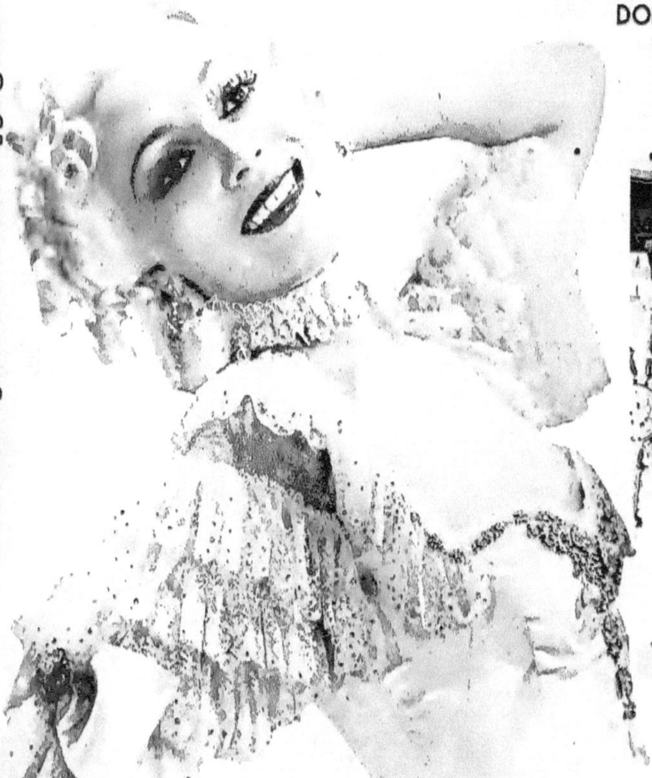

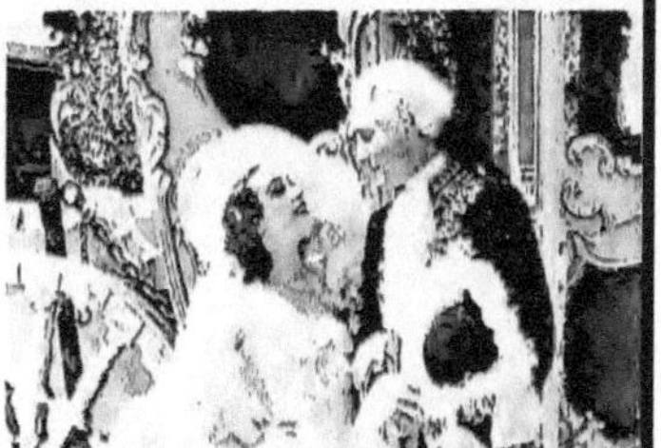

Dolores Del Rio's vivacious fire is ideally suited to the title rôle. She is seen here in a bit of romantic byplay with Victor Jory, the Duc d'Aguillon

TOO MUCH MONEY! That has been Dolores Del Rio's astounding drawback in Hollywood! Now that she again possesses a long-term starring contract which keeps her working regularly once more, she has to fight this extraordinary handicap of hers with even greater vigor.

If she ever relents, gives in to this nigh-unbelievable menace, her career is doomed. And Dolores wants so very much to go on!

Every star in pictures has had some sort of obstacle to overcome. Many have had to deliberately acquire a camera face, and gilding basicly average looks is no easy job. Drastic dieting has been the steady fate of some. Learning to wear clothes with a provocative air has been the task of others. Those who have sprung from unpretentious backgrounds wage a continuous struggle for a convincing veneer of elegance and culture. Since sound, the fine voice requirement has been a familiar stumbling-block.

But the case of Dolores Del Rio is absolutely unparalleled.

She has been remarkably successful in spite of never having known the need for money! If you will check carefully, the driving force which has spurred practically every other star on has been desire for the wealth which the films lavish on their topnotchers.

You have often read of ambitious girls and men being slowed down in Hollywood because they lacked funds. Have you ever heard of a movie actress being impeded by too much money? Yet this, nevertheless, is the only thing which has stood in the lovely Del Rio's path!

Dolores has been wealthy, both before she became famous and ever since. What would seem marvelous luck has, actually, hampered her.

● "As an actress—not personally, of course," she hastens to explain. "So far as my personal life is concerned, being well-to-do has enabled me to elude financial worries. Money has given me much hap-

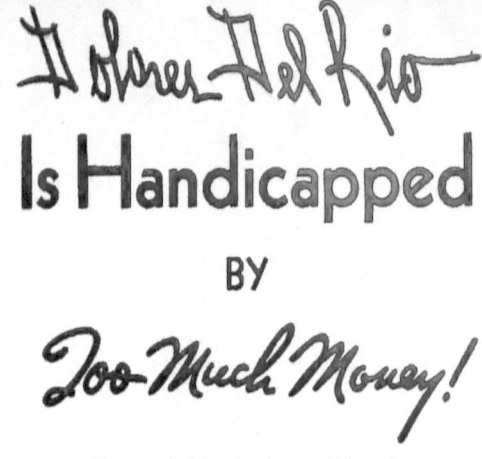

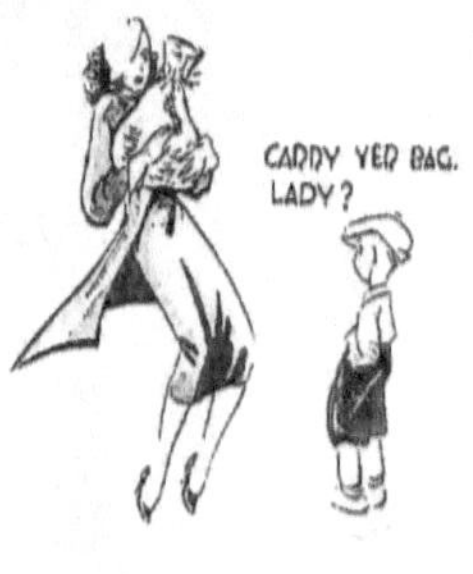

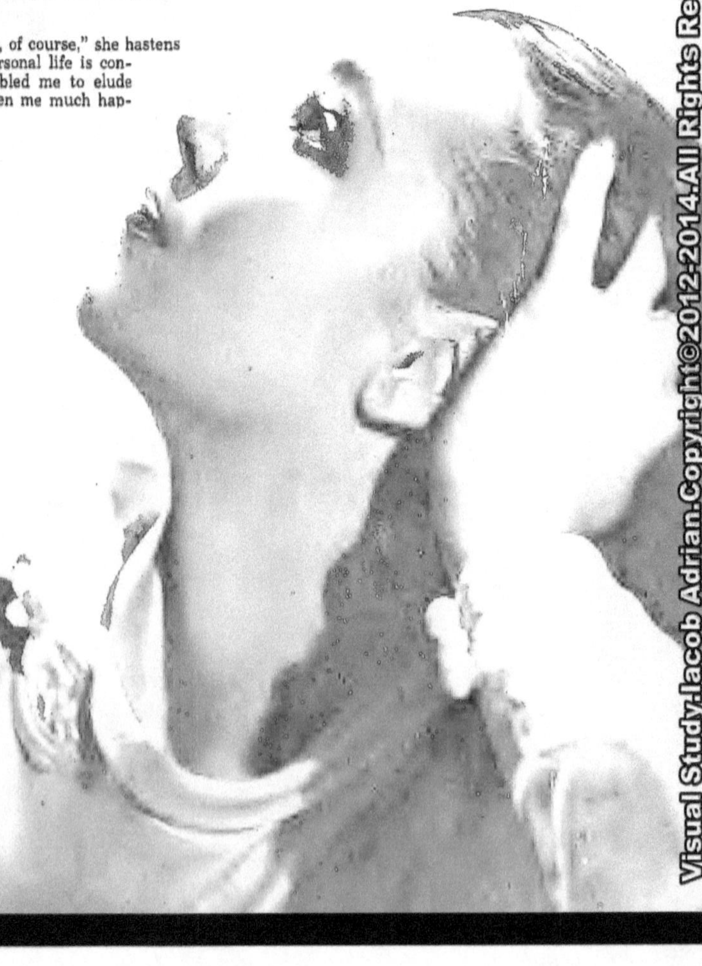

Dolores Del Rio
Is Handicapped
BY
Too Much Money!

How Dolores Del Rio has had to fight relentlessly against a boon that became a curse!

by BEN MADDOX

CARRY YER BAG, LADY?

"As a factor in getting ahead in Hollywood having money has certainly been anything but helpful," says Dolores Del Rio. "Now I know the best training for an actress is hardship"

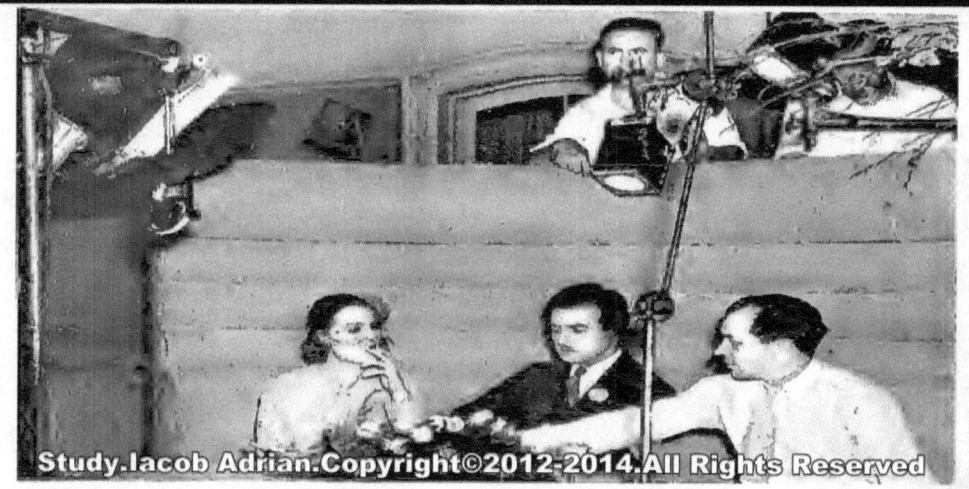

Whitney Bourne, New York socialite who makes her film début in Crime Without Passion; *Claude Rains, who plays the lead, and Charles MacArthur, who is producing and directing it with Ben Hecht, chat on the set while lights are adjusted*

Handicapped by Too Much Money!

piness in allowing me to live comfortably, luxuriously. No woman could deny the pleasure in that!

"However, as a factor in getting ahead in Hollywood having money has certainly been anything but helpful! You might presume that the studios would pay infinitely more attention to you if you came to Hollywood in a 'grand' manner. I can speak with authority, for my own experience taught me differently. When I came here I rented a big place and I entertained extensively. Important, influential producers were my guests and companions.

"They were impressed; yes. But that's all! They liked me and agreed I had good screen possibilities. And right there the interest ceased. Whenever I said I was anxious to work as hard as any girl in town at acting, they laughed. 'You are just fooling,' they insisted. 'You have too much money to be serious, really turn working woman!'"

She hadn't, though. The idea of work had never occurred to her until she bumped into this odd attitude. She had never been crossed and her latent fighting spirit was aroused. Nothing in her former environment or in this annoying Hollywood encouraged Dolores. In fact, she had to combat both the traditional ease to which she'd been accustomed and the snap judgment of the film colony.

"I played four supporting parts before I got my chance at a lead," Dolores tells me. "My money had no bearing on my selection for *What Price Glory?* I did not meet Raoul Walsh, who cast and directed it, until the day I went to take the test for the rôle. I was tested along with half-a-dozen actresses."

She was chosen because she had the best understanding of the part, and because her natural aptitude for emotional acting was evident to Walsh. The public, immediately charmed, demanded more

Del Rio. She had no trouble staying to the fore for more than four years.

GRADUALLY, INSIDIOUSLY, a strange slant to her too-much-money handicap popped up. There was something so lush and gorgeous about her personality that the powers-that-be began branding her "too expensive." Under Edwin Carewe's long supervision each Del Rio release cost nearly a million to make. Which was satisfactory so long as the pictures clicked.

When she was unfortunate enough to get poor stories the feeling grew that she had to rely on an extravagant production set-up. Meanwhile, her salary had mounted startlingly. Once, in the silent era, she was reputedly earning $12,500 a week.

"I was raised to utterly disregard money, to be a wife and mother. My education, at a convent in Mexico City, was instruction in music, literature, and the art of being a worthy housewife.

"At sixteen I married and Jaime and I spent an entire year revelling in the sights of Europe." Although this first marriage of hers went on the rocks after she found fame in Hollywood, she refers to the now-dead Jaime with tenderness.

"I do not regret a moment of that marriage. We were happy. He taught me to appreciate many things. Russian music and art, for instance. I'd never been permitted to read novels. He opened new worlds in countless ways."

Dolores, the intoxicating, is a busy bee these days at Warners. They realize that she doesn't require extravagant bolstering; she has a real following who will flock to see her in worthy stories, the latest of which is *Farewell to Shanghai.* She's conscientiously making herself step as lively as anyone on the lot, vowing never to be permanently daunted by her unique handicap!

DEL RIO BECOMES A STAR REPORTER

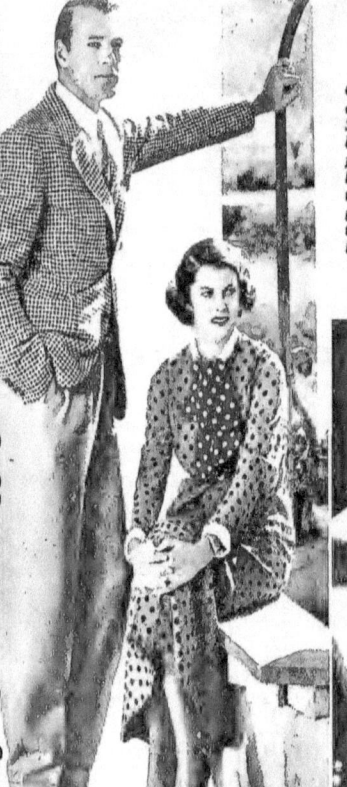

Gary Cooper and his wife, Sandra Shaw, both intimate friends of Dolores' are pictured on the grounds of their ranch home near Hollywood

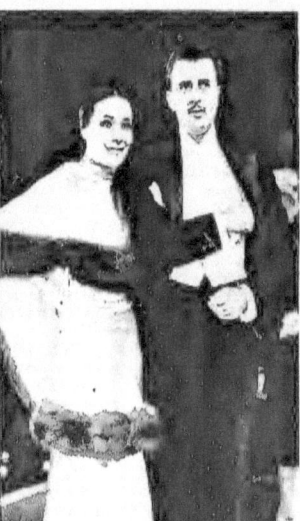

Dolores Del Rio and her husband, Cedric Gibbons, attending a Hollywood party. They are a very vital part of Filmland society

things and the adaptability of modern art design. Side by side these quaint little business cottages glitter in the sunshine, looking for all the world like some architect's dream of the perfect village street.

These early American, English, Monterey, Colonial, Normandy and Dutch cottages are stamped with the individuality which is Hollywood. They are offices . . . shops . . . restaurants. . . .

One of the nearest to Hollywood in the district, and one of the smartest, is the little white Trocadero . . . restaurant par excellence . . . and it was here on a recent night that my husband, Cedric Gibbons, and I, went to a party which was hosted by Carey Wilson, hostessed by Carmelita Geraghty Wilson, and attended by Fay Wray and John Monk Saunders, Gary and Sandra Cooper and ourselves.

ALTHOUGH I HAD been in Mexico but a few weeks my friends graciously gave me a "welcome home" upon my return as enthusiastic as though I'd been gone for a much longer time.

I was delighted with the lovely cocktail party given in my honor by Mr. and Mrs. Wells Root. It became a dinner party, as many such parties do, and we chatted of everything under the sun — the outcome of all the conversation being the decision to fly to Mexico City some week-end to see a bull fight! It is only ten hours to Mexico City by plane now.

Joan Bennett and Gene Markey, Fay Wray and John Monk Saunders, Gary Cooper and Sandra Shaw were among the enthusiasts —We shall see!

FOLLOWING OUR OWN "at home" after my return from Mexico, Sandra and Gary Cooper, Irene and David Selznick, Jean Harlow and Bill Powell and my husband, Cedric Gibbons, and I went to the Clover Club for dinner.

We were lured by the famous cuisine of George Lamaze, the charming singing of lovely Eadie Adams, and the rollicking entertainment of Endor and Farrell, past masters of the art of harmony and rhythm.

One of the most attractive dining rooms in town, ultramodern in design, boasting a glass dance floor, it is a popular rendezvous.

Carole Lombard was there . . . evidencing again that splendid understanding heart which has won so much admiration for her. She and Lansing Brown sat at a nearby table. No romance note for the gossip columns. Just two friends of the late Russ Columbo. The girl helping the

THREE THOUSAND miles from the grey man-made canyons of Park Avenue, which we all know is synonymous with ultra-smartness, Hollywood has quietly and surely developed a smartness of its own. Impossible as it would be to bring the cold sophistication of the East to the sundrenched hills of our famous village, a more informal sophistication has made Hollywood's own personality and culture. This is seen in the mushroom growth of a section along Sunset Boulevard, once a long road skirting the foothills to Beverly Hills, which is now a beehive of business activity.

Business is carried on behind the appealing facades of charming examples of cottage architecture, proving our realization of the demands of the times for beauty in all

In this chatty, revealing article, a charming star gives you an intimate closeup of the Hollywood social scene—takes you to the stars' parties, tells you what they eat, what they wear and who they're seen with—and where

by *Dolores Del Rio*

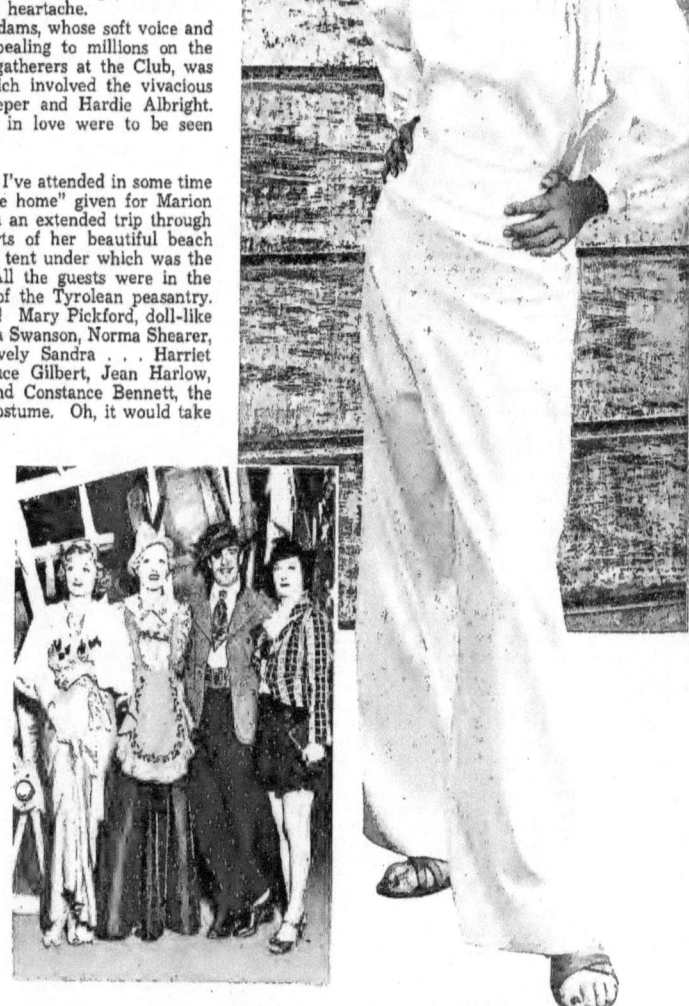

boy to pick up the shattered pieces of his life—a life weighted by the sorrow which has been Lansing's since that fateful Sunday when the gun in his hand discharged a bullet to ricochet crazily across the room and still forever the voice of his friend. There, in that gay little room was that poignant reminder of heartache.

Applauding the slim Eadie Adams, whose soft voice and quiet beauty would be as appealing to millions on the screen as it is to the nightly gatherers at the Club, was Glenda Farrell in a party which involved the vivacious Alice Brady . . . Martha Sleeper and Hardie Albright. Young newlyweds very much in love were to be seen dancing.

THE LARGEST and gayest party I've attended in some time was the wonderful "welcome home" given for Marion Davies, who just returned from an extended trip through Europe. The two tennis courts of her beautiful beach house were covered by a large tent under which was the gayest of Tyrolean villages. All the guests were in the quaint and colorful costumes of the Tyrolean peasantry.

And just everyone was there! Mary Pickford, doll-like in her simple costume . . . Gloria Swanson, Norma Shearer, Gary Cooper and the shy, lovely Sandra . . . Harriet Parsons, lily-like Virginia Bruce Gilbert, Jean Harlow, the Donald Ogden Stewarts and Constance Bennett, the only guest who did not wear costume. Oh, it would take more pages than I have here to list the many guests!

Under the spell of the setting and the costumes we were much like children . . . dancing folk dances to the strains of German music, which was played exclusively, and parading in two's about the "village." Everyone agreed that it was *the* party of the season. And the graciousness which has made Marion Davies so beloved by her friends was never more in evidence than that evening when everyone of the numerous guests was made to feel so delightfully at home.

THEN THERE was the Russian party given to honor the Prince and Princess Vasili Romanoff by the Frank Tuttles. The Prince is the nephew of the late Czar of Russia and he and the Princess, with the beautiful dignified courage of the erstwhile Russian aristocracy, made me conscious of a deep regret that the color, pageantry and gaiety of the old

Hollywood's most unique social affair was the Tyrolean party given by Marion Davies upon her return from Europe. Left to right, Constance Bennett, Marion Davies, Raoul Walsh and Countess di Frasso

The glamorous Dolores Del Rio is one of the inner circle in Hollywood's exclusive society. Her comments on these pages take you with her on a round of social gayety

Del Rio Becomes a Star Reporter

Russia is no more. We danced to the strains of gypsy music, first rollicking, then sad, ever carrying the beat which is so peculiarly Russian. We ate great helpings of Russian food. And there were many stories of heroic survival told that night! Jean Harlow was there with Bill Powell . . . I almost said "as usual" . . . King Vidor escorted Betty Hill . . . lovely intense looking young Katherine De Mille was there, as was Jack Gilbert, who, as usual, came alone. Jack has gone everywhere alone since his divorce from Virginia Bruce.

It was a most charming party. All the way to my home in Santa Monica, and all through the next day the strains of the gypsy music lingered in my mind . . . and my admiration for the Prince and Princess is indeed great.

Gary and Sandra, Cedric and I, often dine at the Russian Eagle. Here the genial General Lodijensky, one time of the Imperial Russian Army, is host. Blini is our favorite dish. Now blini may not sound an impressive thing to eat, but it is! Impressively delicious. It is crepes . . . thin little pancakes piled high with spreadings of caviar and covered with gobs of sour cream! No diet order, this. But how the four of us love it! Marlene Dietrich is a regular diner there . . . as is the fragile looking Lilian Harvey who is always squired by Director Paul Martin. Garbo, too, sometimes enjoys the hospitality of the Lodijenskys. Mr. and Mrs. Richard Dix, who are one of the happiest looking couples I've seen in a good long time; the Ralph Bellamys, just back from a real vacation trip to England, the John Mack Browns, Kathleen Howard and Adrian, all were there the other night.

The Russian influence has invaded the fashions too! Swagger, flaring wide-belted coat suits, the lines of which are not unlike those worn by the Cossacks, are being seen more and more. These ensembles are topped by turbans of purest Russian line. They have a rakish quality which has long been missing in the mode.

Lunch Time at the Vendome! Wally Beery, genial, devoted to his little girl, Carol Ann, who is his constant companion, surrounded by a group of laughing friends . . . Gene Raymond passing from booth to booth greeting friends and finally joining my little luncheon party to reminisce about the good times our company had making *Flying Down to Rio* . . . The Countess di Frasso, resplendent in the latest Hattie Carnegie model of royal purple, wearing a cape and carrying a muff made of the breasts of humming birds! . . . Proving that feathers, which have had small place in fashions for some seasons, are "in" this winter. She, too, stopped at my table to show us the lovely sketches made by Elsa de Wolfe, noted New York decorator who is to do the new house which the Countess is building in California. . . . Sylvia Sidney, in a smart brown ensemble, at one table; Adolphe Menjou, in makeup, at another; the reconciled Ben and Ad Schulberg greeting friends across the room . . . And at the round table, Walter Wanger, Edwin Schallert and others . . . Lewis Milestone, Myron

Selznick, deep in a discussion in the next booth . . . And the blonde Virginia Bruce was there in an exquisite soft blue outfit.

At the Beverly Brown Derby, John McCormick and Margaret Sullavan greet friends who pause to talk with them. . . . Charles Furthman recounts the thrill he had when his automobile was washed from the road during our first heavy rainstorm . . . Joan Bennett and Margaret Ettinger are an attractive duo farther along the room . . . Rene Borzage, the attractive wife of Frank Borzage, attired in riding clothes, stops in for a bit of luncheon on her way back from the polo field . . . Alan Hale, whose artistry is receiving the recognition it deserves, comes in . . . Alan has been making three pictures at one time for the past month. He has skyrocketed ever since his fine performance in *Little Man What Now*.

The Most Fun I had during the month was on the duck-hunting trip the Gary Coopers, Cedric and I took over one week-end. We went to our usual secluded spot and returned tired, dirty and triumphant with a fine brace of ducks.

The old argument between our two menfolks arose. The argument as to which home boasts the better cook! We decided to settle it once and for all by the simple expedient of dividing the spoils of the hunt, eating at our house one night and at Gary and Sandra's the next.

Faithfully we followed the plan. And the gallant husbands who were to be the final judges made it a draw! Gary politely saying our cook won and Cedric politely affirming the victory of the Cooper chef! But Sandra and I are sure that the argument is not settled!

It Has Been a busy month—but I shall be busier next month when I go to work in my next picture *In Caliente*.

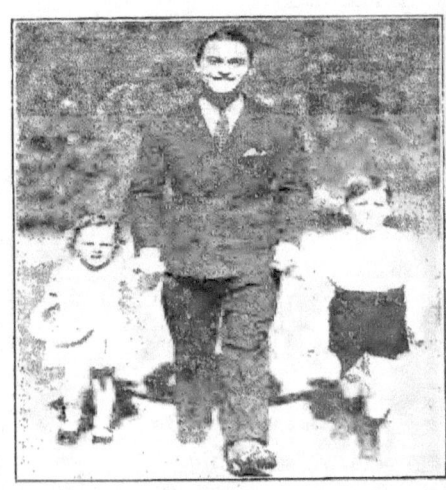

Off for an ice cream! Chester Morris, Universal star, with his two children

Script

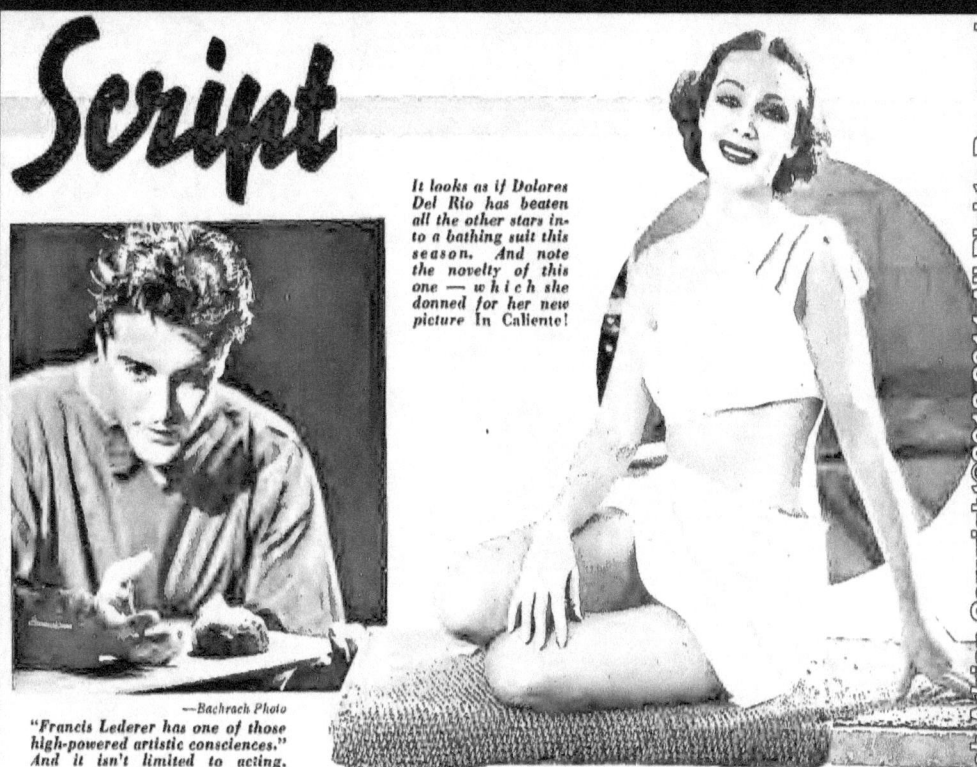

It looks as if Dolores Del Rio has beaten all the other stars into a bathing suit this season. And note the novelty of this one — w h i c h she donned for her new picture In Caliente!

—Bachrach Photo

"Francis Lederer has one of those high-powered artistic consciences." And it isn't limited to acting, either. He has recently taken up sculpturing as a hobby

The Harlow Handwriting

ONE OF THESE handwriting experts (they are all famous since the Hauptmann case) tells me that the girl with the most real character in Hollywood is Jean Harlow. She has the courage and adaptability to tackle anything and make a success of it. The expert has it that Jean should have been the most successful of any of them in married life, as she has sympathy and tolerance.

Big Dan and Little Lionel

TO SEE LIONEL BARRYMORE as the rough, bluff *Dan Peggotty* on the screen, and then see him on the street fills one with amazement.

In the rôle, he looks big enough and strong enough to bite lamp posts off with his teeth. In real life, he is a slight man, a man of delicate health.

Two on Their Way Up

THERE ARE TWO players who seem to have won tickets to any heights to which they want to go.

One is Margo, who gave such an astonishing performance in *Crime Without Passion;* and the other is Freddie Bartholomew, the little boy who was *David Copperfield* in the first part of the picture.

Margo's latest assignment in pictures was as a dancer in *Rumba*, which was

She Done Us Wrong

THE MYSTERY ABOUT Mae West's racing stable has been cleared up. She has four or five horses, but they are trotters. I am disappointed. A trotter isn't a horse; it is a phenomenon of Nature. More was expected of Mae.

Glutton for Punishment

MY IDEA OF a game guy is a director who would take on Francis Lederer and Katharine Hepburn in the same picture. *Break of Hearts* was a good name for it.

Wholesale murder was avoided when Lederer stepped out in favor of Charles Boyer.

Lederer is a charming fellow, but he has one of those high-powered artistic consciences—like von Stroheim. It is utterly impossible for him to do anything to which he is not sold from the heart out.

not so hot . . . but not her fault. You will be hearing from her again. The man-child will be in as much demand as any actor in Hollywood for the rest of this year. If he lasts beyond that, he can pin a miracle medal on himself. Little girls occasionally grow up to be stars; but little boy-stars seem to grow down. I can't think of a half-dozen who ever grew up and got anywhere.

Schnozzle Is Recluseful

SCHNOZZLE DURANTE has forsaken the ways of men and society. He is seen out at parties about as little as any actor in Hollywood. He says he gets tired of being expected to "act up" all the time. The truth is he has never been the hit in pictures that he and everyone else expected. And I don't know why. Perhaps because he is essentially a lone wolf. His best stuff is impromptu and alone.

Napoleon on the Way?

SOONER OR LATER, Edward G. Robinson, Charlie Chaplin or Ernst Lubitsch will get Napoleon on the screen and we shall get it over with. They have all had the itch for years. Now Lubitsch, as boss of the works at Paramount, can have his own way.

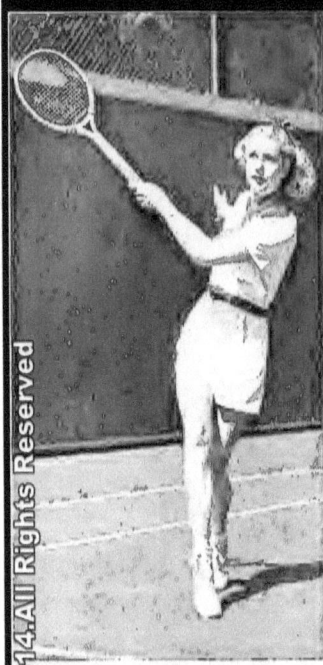
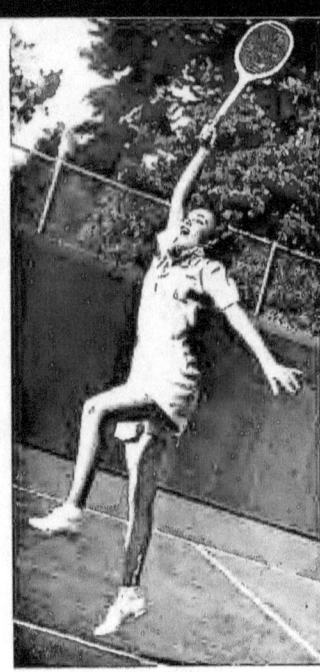

A Study in LIGHT and DARK

Blonde and brunette, Anita Louise and Dolores Del Rio make an interesting contrast of types as they play tennis in sunny Hollywood!

by
CHARLES
RHODES

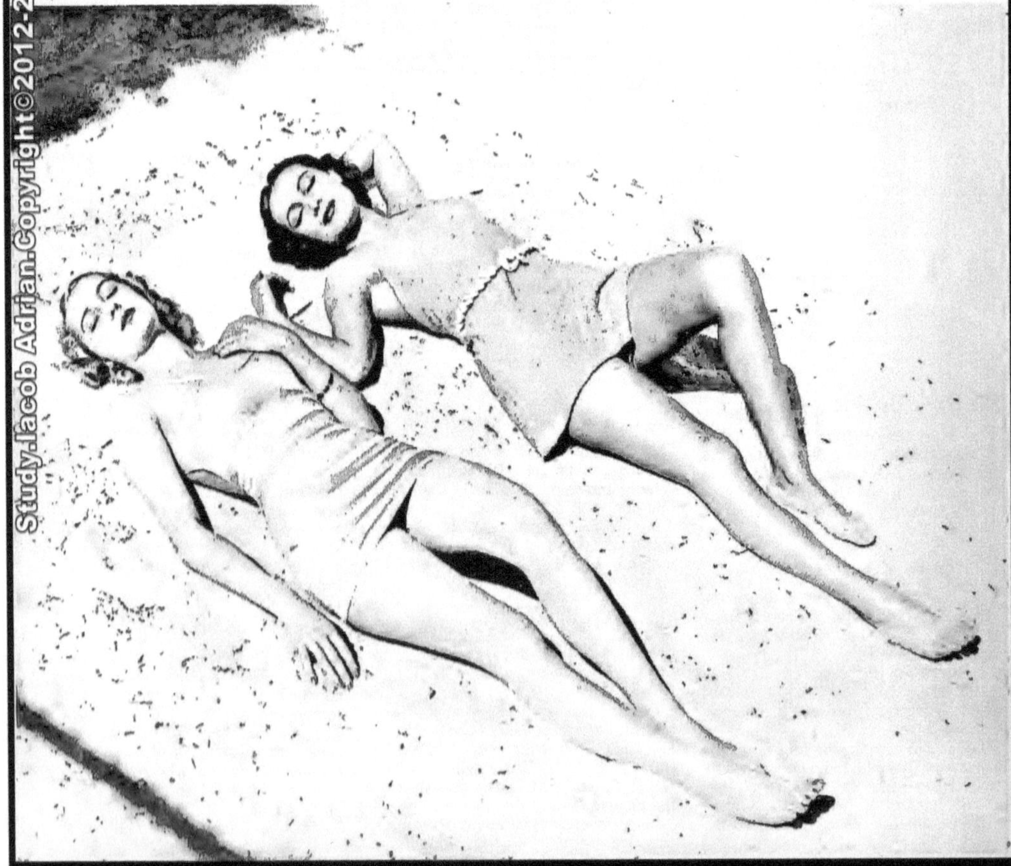

Dolores Del Rio—Always A Lady!

MORE THAN ANYTHING ELSE, Dolores Del Rio is a lady. Occasionally there are trying times when Hollywood stars remember—or forget—such a status according to their individual abilities. But femininity, grace and beauty are synonymous with Del Rio, and never to be questioned.

Nevertheless, one morning recently in New York harbor the question did arise, and only the innate human understanding which Dolores possesses saved the day.

She was just arriving back in America on the huge British liner *Queen Mary*. It was the end of a three month business trip to London where she had been doing a starring rôle in *Accused*.

The *Queen Mary* arrived in port on its second trip amid a great hub-bub. Whistles shrieked out from excited tug-boats. On shore, as on its maiden voyage, thousands of people watched from every possible vantage point. Newspaper men climbed aboard with a busy air of importance.

In her cabin Dolores Del Rio slept on, unaware of the ballyhoo without. Suddenly a dozen fists smashed against her door. Lovely Dolores awoke with a start, cried out, "What is it, please?" (She had visions of a terrible catastrophe, of another *Titanic*. She was, in a word, scared silly.)

"We're the press!" someone shouted. "Open up!"

Dolores, clad only in negligee, stammered her answer.

"I am frightfully sorry! I am just awakening. I am not dressed. Presently I shall be glad to see you!"

From without the door was blustering. "Come out whether you are dressed or not. Do you think we enjoy getting up at six in the morning? Don't go Hollywood on us. We're very busy. Lots of people to see."

Dolores was about to say, "Why don't you go see them, then?" with a stamp of her fluffy slippers. Instead she remem-

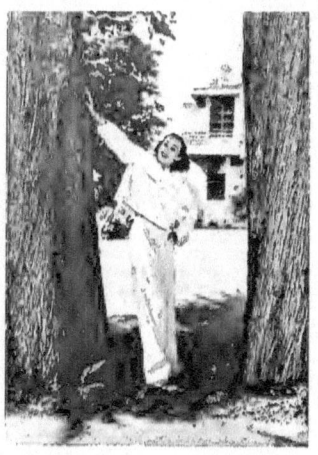
Two giant pines, twins 200 years old, shade the lawn alongside the modernistic home

bered that she always had been a very feminine lady, and replied, "I am so sorry. Soon I will be ready. Please have patience." And Dolores dressed quickly. Rude as the press representatives had been, Del Rio was graciousness itself.

It can be recorded here that she spent the ensuing two hours walking up and down stairs, posing for cameramen and giving interviews. All with a smile. And for what? So that a couple of newspapers could give those aloof sort of interviews that reveal the reporter's cold disapproval. Dolores would have felt pretty unhappy about it all if a couple of the ship reporters had not come to her and apologized for the conduct of the group. And when, later, there appeared a story criticizing her for keeping her waiting, she still said nothing.

Dolores Del Rio acted like a lady because she is first of all a woman. A gracious, human, utterly feminine woman.

The Screen Does Not Flatter

● THIS EXOTIC YOUNG WOMAN from the land of the dons has so much more than beauty. Believe us, the screen reproduces but never flatters Del Rio. She is, with her warm gold skin, her wide dark eyes in their thick fringe of silken lashes, her blue-black hair, her slender patrician hands, her perfect contour of face and figure, the perfect beauty. She plays with years and laughs at them.

She lived the cloistered childhood of old Spain. Nor has she entirely forgotten it in the modern surroundings of the home her husband, Cedric Gibbons, designed for her. We want to tell you about that home, because it reflects the modern femininity of Del Rio as you know her, yet retains a touch of the old atmosphere of her ancestors.

Dolores' home is down by the sea in Santa Monica canyon. You need a map and a slide rule to find it, but once you have spotted the chromium gates at the end of the winding road, you have come to a modern little palace.

A butler greets you at the door. If your visit is kosher, he presses a button and the

gate opens. You are ushered into a gleaming white reception room, with creamy white rugs. Soon you find that every room has these thick, velvety rugs. But while you wait the butler goes up winding, modern stairs to announce your presence.

Off to the right you catch a glimpse of the dining room, not large but distinctly different. Most eyecatching is the crystal top table, hard enough to resist the blow from a bludgeon. There is nothing gaudy about this room. Rather, it is cool and restful and unobtrusive.

She Loves Books Around Her

● PRESENTLY WE CLIMB the long stairs and find ourselves in the drawing room, again with white walls and rugs. The book cases are of rust lacquer, and you know instantly that Dolores and her husband like books for what they contain. There are very few sets of books in immaculate order. Instead, we find scores and scores of novels, biographies and other non-fiction books, each proud of its own niche.

In the center is a chromium and black fireplace, screened with a curtain of chromium mesh. Dolores sits in front of it, sipping an iced glass of grape juice. She is wearing a white jacket over a red dress. Designers could tell you something interesting and different about her simple clothes. All we know is that the effect is pleasing and extremely fitting.

Dolores has just come in from an auto ride along the ocean which you can see from the window, basking in the afternoon sun. But she did not do the driving.

"I love to ride horseback," she tells us smilingly, "but it is different trying to manage a car. Imagine it—I have not the slightest idea what to do with all the wheels and things in an automobile! I would be frightened beyond words at the thought of driving. And it is so dangerous in Los Angeles!"

Then who does do the driving, we inquire.

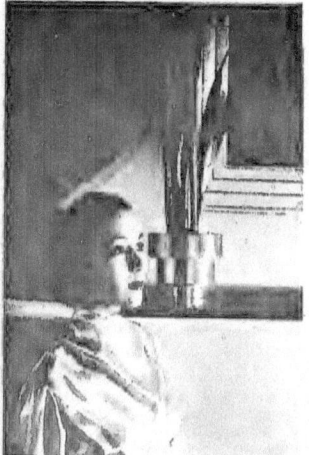
Everything in her house, like Dolores herself, is a study in light and dark, brilliance and shadow. Hence, chromium and black furnishings adorn the mantels, the bookcases

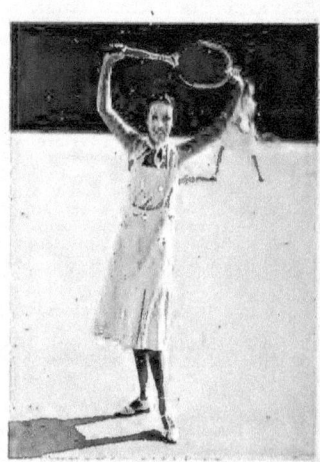
Del Rio finds tennis good fun, but she is not an expert. Women can afford to be merely decorative in this game, she maintains

Dolores Del Rio—Always a Lady

"My very good chauffeur who has been with me for years. Or Ceddie (Cedric Gibbons, her husband). It doesn't matter which. Both of them drive divinely. I love to ride when Cedric is at the wheel. But I shall never drive if I can help it!"

She admires men and what they do. She clings to them from inclination, not necessity. But she does not envy them.

"Why are girls today so proud of doing all the things which men have done for centuries? I do not envy men. Nothing is more thrilling than being a woman in a man's world. Why must they try to change it?"

Softly, plaintively, with a show of pity for the modern girl, she asks her question.

Her boudoir is the perfect setting for its feminine occupant. All silver and white and crystal. The bed clings low to the floor, in modernistic style. Everything is modern and gleaming—everything but a tiny shrine in which a candle, lighted from the eternal flame, burns softly.

An Amazing Dressing Room

⬤ HER DRESSING ROOM is something to make you gasp. It is of silver and white, with mirrors gleaming everywhere. A dressing table built low, banks up to the left and right in tiers. On its various levels are a hundred bottles of exquisite perfume.

Rows upon rows of dainty wearing apparel are behind the silver doors of the closets behind you. You won't find any slacks there, nor sports trousers, nor even a mannishly tailored street suit.

The bath is a dream. Black tile shows where there is room for it. Most of the wall space is an astonishing array of mirrors. You see yourself not once but a hundred times, from dozens of facets.

"These aren't vanity mirrors," Dolores explains. "They just give you a thoroughgoing look at yourself. You can't see only that favorite angle. You see every one of your faults. Mirrors keep your ego in place."

She plays a desultory game of tennis . . . but looks like an angel in motion as she springs with grace, but little accuracy, about the court. Once, a friend, with a bit of exasperation in her tone, said, "Dolores, you really should take a few lessons!"

"Why?" laughing from behind her lashes, "Why? Do I not look well enough on the court? Ah, do you really, truly believe, my lovely friend, that the men WANT us to beat them at this game? It is their game. Let them play it. Let them enjoy their smiles at my efforts with it. It is too strenuous for women anyway!"

She swims gracefully, daintily, with a quiet enthusiasm, and is devastatingly decorative as she sits in a trim white silk suit on the edge of the pool. She abhors bridge, but admits she loves conversation.

"I love to gossip. I simply adore to gossip." Pure mischief shines in her eyes at this confession comes forth on a tiny crescendo of laughter. "Only I always get it mixed up . . . so I don't do it much. But I do love it!"

Handling an Enemy

⬤ SHE HAS AN ENTIRELY feminine angle on the way to handle an enemy without deliberately adding malice. " 'Let them alone,' I say to myself. 'Poor things!'

The meanest thing one can do to an enemy is . . . do nothing. If you ignore an enemy long enough, who knows? He may become a friend in self-defense! No one likes being ignored, you know."

The very unreasonableness of this argument makes it reasonable. There are those who will swear to you that Dolores always has her own way. I know this is not so. But I know, too, that it seems to be so because of the feminine psychology which she applies to her living.

She is resourceful sometimes to a delightful degree in doing things her own way.

Every woman's prerogative—change of mind, she employs with divine extravagance. Once she and Cedric had planned an out-of-town week-end together far in advance of the date set. With the pressure of social and studio activities, neither had mentioned the plan for weeks. On a Friday, the night they were to leave, when Cedric arrived home, Dolores greeted him in formal dinner gown. "But dear, your traveling suit, we're pulling out, aren't we?" Cedric asked.

Dolores smiled brightly. "Oh, but darling—but didn't I tell you? I changed our minds. We'll go next week instead. You don't mind?"

Cedric didn't mind. The unexpected charms this young Irishman. Calmly he walked upstairs, changed to dinner clothes, and greeted some twenty guests as though he had planned just THIS for weeks.

And what about frankness in women? "Pooh! Why, frankness is so often rude! Since when must women be frank? I like to follow the pattern set down for women through the ages. Mystery is incomparably more alluring than frankness."

Contentment Comes First

⬤ WITH A TRUE FEMININE instinct, she wants peace and happiness about her. She wants her friends to be gay and content. That is why she never argues for anything. Rather, she most charmingly appears to relinquish her opinions in deference to others. In reality she quietly tucks them away to be used on another day!

"I am entirely honest when I say to you, I am glad I am a woman. I am proud that I have all, and I mean every single one of the funny, unreasonable faults of my feminine ancestors. I like to have my own way. But I can be patient about it. I don't care how foolish that way may seem. Somehow I don't even care if Cedric sometimes gives me my way with a very real annoyance at its unreasonableness. That is much better than winning a brisk, sexless argument because my mind worked like a machine. Because I was logical, and sane, and proved the mathematics of my point.

"Just because this is a machine age . . . because steel and wire and engines are becoming more and more important in the scheme of things, must women take on the coloration of the times?

"Naturally, I can't answer for the modern women, but I can answer for myself. And I answer 'No,' very definitely.

"Perversity is a feminine trait, you know, and so, as I see women becoming more and more imbued with the ideas of adopting the rules and behavior of men, I become more and more determined to be myself."

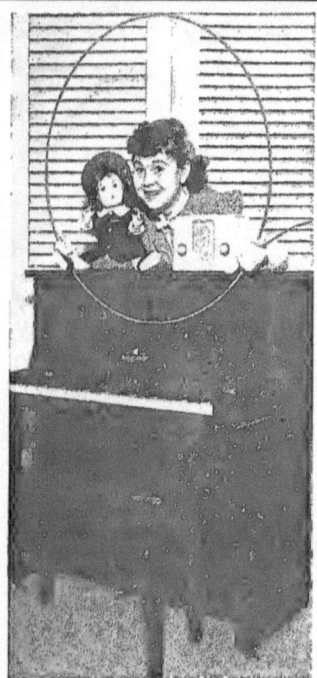

Jane Withers smiles over the top of the miniature piano which she will present to the clever winner of her "Miss Santa Claus" contest. Second prize is the pretty little radio, and third is the Jane Withers doll. The hoop, Jane is keeping for herself. Because of the great number of answers, winners will not be announced until next month's issue

For OUR GANG simply dotes on it ... now.

THE GANG, it seems, was summoned to the studio to make some Thanksgiving pictures for publicity purposes. "Aw," they grumped, "it's nuthin' but a lotta hooey ... prop turkeys and no fun."

But a surprise awaited them. The pictures were to be made in color. And as color picks up as black-and-white does not, real food had to be used.

Presto, chango ... roasted brown turkeys made their appearance, with cranberry sauce and pies and all the wotnots that accompany a turkey dinner! The kids have been clamoring for more publicity pictures ever since.

█ A letter from M A U R E E N O'SULLIVAN, now in England playing the leading feminine role in A Yank At Oxford, discloses that she and husband-JOHN FARROW are living in a small cottage in the town of Denham, only a few minutes' walk from the studio ... and the house was built in 1561.

Further . . . the entire troupe uses elaborate trailers for dressing rooms. And, one day, while motoring through the country at a leisurely pace, she chanced to look behind and there were fifteen or sixteen people on bicycles following her. When they saw she noticed them, all—as of one accord—waved to her.

█ W. S. VAN DYKE, the director, delights in baiting people. NELSON EDDY is his latest victim.

A certain woman writer for an important syndicate wrote something about the two that neither particularly liked. They got together, and agreed that neither would henceforth have anything to do with this individual, and they'd make things as tough as possible for her.

Came the day she arrived on the set. "I won't work with that women here," EDDY declared. He stalked away for a few moments, then returned.

There, chatting and laughing uproariously, sat VAN DYKE and the writer, the best of friends. EDDY, now, trusts NO ONE.

█ LITTLE LOOK-SEES: H A R O L D LLOYD is taking unto himself new fame, as The Great Clayton. In the event this title means nothing to you ... LLOYD has turned mind-reader—for social purposes, of course—but it's reported that his talent along this line is positively amazing.

CONSTANCE BENNETT has gone into the cosmetics business, and you'll probably be using her product yourself before long. Her brand is shortly to go on the market in every prominent city of the United States.

OLIVER HARDY, of LAUREL and HARDY, can't play Bridge unless there's a platter—yes, platter—of sandwiches by his side. Whenever he enters a game at the club, a waiter always hovers near to see that the platter is never empty.

FRANCES LANGFORD has started a "friendship garden" along the side of her new Brentwood home. It will be used exclusively for flowers and plants given her by her friends. Already, there are more than fifty different varieties of rare plants.

FRED ASTAIRE has copyrighted the Drum Dance he has devised for Damsel In Distress. More than twenty drums of rather mammoth proportions are used in this sequence, and 'tis reported it is one of the most novel dancing numbers ever viewed.

.

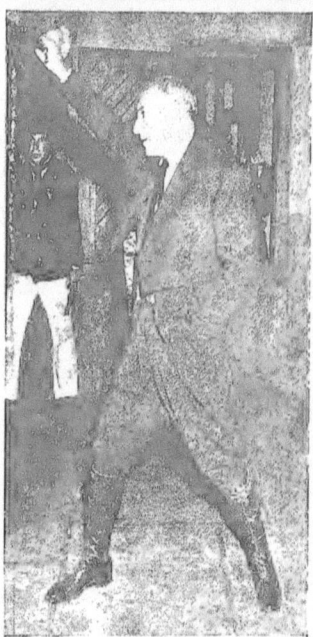

Norma Shearer, just beginning to appear in public again, greets Dolores Del Rio and Gregory Ratoff before a Philharmonic concert

As usual, Cecil De Mille does as much acting as anyone in the cast of the film he is producing. Here he is in full action, testing the steel of a sword to be used by Fredric March in his role of the c o l o r f u l pirate, La Fitte, in The Buccaneer. He borrowed the 19th century tail coat from his star to help him get in the proper swash-buckling mood

█ Because she failed to heed the warning of a studio make-up artist, LILY PONS found herself immersed in trouble.

For several of the scenes in her latest picture, Lily had to wear body make-up. A new type of make-up was used, one on which water had no effect. A special remover was required to divest the wearer of this make-up. Moreover, water turned the make-up into a hard cake, and almost impossible to remove.

Well, sir, Lily forgot all about this, and when the day's work was done dashed to her dressing room and under the shower. And therein lies our tale.

Three women labored over Lily for more than an hour, in an effort to remove the cakey substance that covered almost her entire body. Lily, at last reports, had put herself completely in the hands of her make-up artist.

█ Shades of CECIL B. DE MILLE ... bathtubs have come into their own again. You'll see MIRIAM HOPKINS in one, in Women Have a Way and GLADYS SWARTHOUT, too, in Romance in the Dark. Miriam spent three days completely immersed—well, all but her head—and what a time ...

10 WAYS TO AVOID MATRIMONY

George Sanders does not claim to be a Don Juan or a more than normally pursued young man, but here is how he learned about the single life the hard way

By MELISSA DODD

"Ten ways to avoid matrimony . . ." ruminated George Sanders, his six feet three of height outlined against the stone chimney in the living room, has gray-green eyes humorous, "I wonder if there's anything a man needs to know more in these expensive days than how not to get married? Well, I know ten ways.

"I learned them in Finland, Denmark, Germany, France, England and South America. Unintentionally, mind you."

He ran a hand across thick brown hair in a rueful gesture. He is, of course, the hero of *The Life of A Lancer Spy*, a picture in which he plays no less than four (please count 'em!) roles. He was the film husband, a meanie, of Madeleine Carroll in *Lloyd's of London*, and subsequently had parts in *Slave Ship* and *Love Is News*.

In short, Sanders—you pronounce it "Sahnders," for it's as English as Piccadilly Circus—is the new discovery at 20th Century-Fox Studios. They don't understand why the personable young man hasn't been marched to the altar long before this. But Sanders understands, all right.

Not that he's a woman hater; he simply isn't a woman seeker. He just reads and smokes his pipe and sails a boat at the studio. His big ambition is to snaffle 20 hours' sleep a day but, failing this, he snaffles as much as he can. He even lives in solitude at the top of a gosh-awful hill on a road called, aptly, Hermit's Glen.

"In avoiding matrimony," continued the hermit of Hermit's Glen, his raffish look belying the modulated accents, "a man generally has to be skillful. But I wasn't. My single blessedness, if it's that, comes from following rules I didn't know existed. Like that time about the silver box.

"And a good thing! For if a man marries too early, he's likely to marry the wrong woman.

"Meanwhile, you behold in me an expert. An inadvertent expert. From my own sad experiences and those of my friends I've gleaned ten rules on how

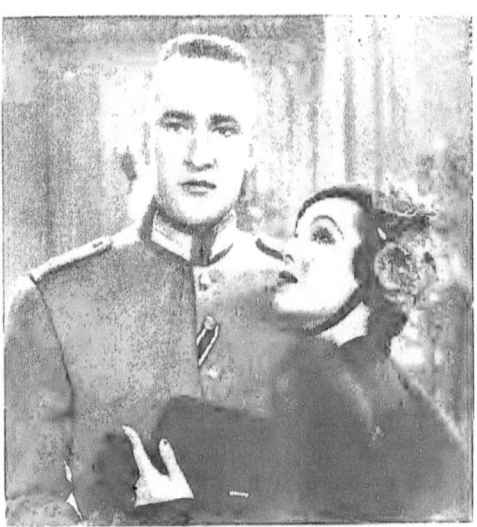

George Sanders shows of what stern stuff he is made in *The Life of a Lancer Spy* by resisting the allure of Dolores Del Rio at this moment in the adventure film

to strew the banana peel in the path of romance.

"Curbstones did it in Denmark. A silver box in Venezuela. A hat in Paris."

He slanted an eyebrow from the corner where he'd dropped into a big chair. The knotty pine living room of this neat, camp-like house among eucalyptus trees and terraces of blue-purple flowers has comfortable chairs all about, and plenty of end tables with books on them; a man's room, with a free outlook from many windows down the tumbled green hillside. A bachelor is safe here from at least the damsels who are overweight; they'd be out of breath before the slope was half way conquered, let alone the hermit on top of it.

Don't toss an overabundance of solicitude, however, at the hermit in question. He's around 200 completely athletic pounds; former interscholastic boxing champion during his English college career, after he and his British parents escaped the revolution in Russia where

he happened to have been born; an expert swimmer, holder of the British Humane Society Medal for rescuing a man from the Thames; and, with time out for tobacco growing in Brazil, a London stage, radio and cinema hit.

"Curbstones," the hermit was recalling gloomily; "they have nice, high curbs in some of the towns of Denmark, and I was tired of walking, so I sat down on one. She said people didn't do such things. I grew stubborn, and sat, anyway. I like to sit on curbstones. She walked off, and I never could even get her by telephone afterward. Be highly individualistic (she called it conspicuous!) in conservative company. That's rule No. 1 for the wedding-ring dodger.

"Then—I prefer to sail a boat alone or with a couple of fellows, no woman tottering about the deck. And I like raw onions. If a lady needs a gas mask to listen to your tender chatter (have you any idea how harsh 'gas mask' sounds in Finnish?), or if you never meet girls under glamorous circumstances, the spell of the sea, you know, or the moonlight and whatnot—Well, there you are. Or here I am.

"A fourth way to make an orange blossom curl up, as I realized from watching a friend's effort, is to launch the topic of hard times plus an endorsement of the economic equality of the sexes when the waiter presents the dinner check. My word, that'll work like a charm; she never spoke to him again. Still another method, which unfolded on the Riviera, is to ignore the little amenities. By the time a second friend of mine hadn't done enough hand-kissing and bowing from the waist to suit his lady love—finis! With fireworks."

Sanders puffed thoughtfully at his pipe. "A truly infallible way to scramble the bridal bouquet and make utter hash of the nuptials, though, is to get going about the superiority of the male...

"Kitty Foyle"

The studio met the challenge and found a way to retain the intimacy of the tale. It's done through a trick device in which *Kitty's* other self appears to counsel her, points out her past mistakes and warns her against what she is about to do. This other self engages in discussion with *Kitty* and takes her back over the hectic years of her life since she was a child of fifteen.

First, the Hays office did a bit of white-washing on certain elements in the plot. In the book, *Kitty Foyle* was expecting her lover's baby without benefit of clergy. "Tsk, tsk," said the keepers of our movie morals, "none of that." So, for purposes of purity, *Kitty* is secretly married to *Wyn*, but has the marriage annulled, so the heartbreak is the same.

You're going to be introduced to two new male heart-breakers in *Kitty Foyle*. Dennis Morgan, who isn't exactly new since he has been kicking around Hollywood a few years but not getting beyond minor parts, will make you wonder where he's been all your life. He plays *Kitty's* charming but impressionable society boy friend, *Wyn Strafford*. This is considered one of the prize roles of the year, and you'd be surprised at the prominent male stars who begged for a chance at it.

The other new face is James Craig, who has done little in Hollywood outside of playing in amateur theater groups. He's a tall-dark-and-handsome and a little on the Cary Grant side. Although Dennis is the main male love interest in the picture, it is Craig who finally gets the girl. You won't feel that Ginger—that is, *Kitty*—is being short-changed, either!

Kitty Foyle loves, and is loved by *Wyn Strafford*, a young Philadelphia society man. She meets him when she is fifteen and he becomes an integral part in her stormy life up until the age of twenty-eight.

Wyn is unable to tear away from convention. He is kept under the thumb of his very social Philadelphia family, and *Kitty* is a girl born on the other side of the tracks. She tries to escape *Wyn's* insidious hold on her and the flaming love that almost consumes them. She leaves Philadelphia for Chicago, and then New York.

In New York she gets a job and becomes a member of the gallant and staggering army of twenty million working girls—girls who live in subways, in offices and in one-room-and-percolator apartments. *Kitty* mirrors this generation of modern young working girls, their philosophy, their courage, and their ability to take an emotional jolt and pick up their lives again.

Kitty's life is no bed of roses. She bears *Wyn's* child and sees it die. In the moment when she needs him most, she learns that *Wyn* is being married in a fashionable Philadelphia church to a girl of his own set.

Nevertheless, she can't escape *Wyn*, even after she has met another man who is in love with her. He is *Mark Eisen*, a young interne, played by the handsome Mr. Craig. *Wyn* seeks *Kitty* out in New York, and begs her to go to Europe with him. His wife refuses to give him a divorce, but he promises her continuation of the love that was interrupted before. *Kitty* is still fascinated by him.

The story concludes with *Kitty* facing the most fateful decision of her life—whether to go away to Europe with *Wyn*, or to marry *Mark*, and find respectability and happiness of a sort.

Wyn is at the harbor, waiting for her to meet him and go to Europe with him. *Mark* is at the hospital, waiting for *Kitty* to meet him so that they can run off and be married in Greenwich.

In her room at the Pocahontas Hotel for Women, *Kitty* goes to a mirror, looks at herself gravely, and reminisces her past.

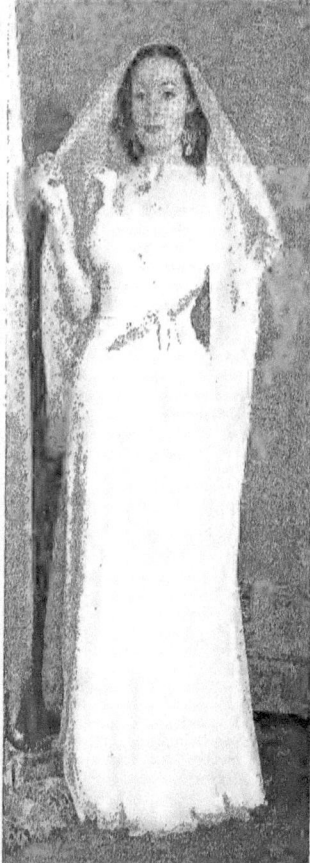

Lovely Dolores Del Rio is shown in an exclusive "Irene" model, a white chiffon formal gown with a gold and white silk bird embroidered on the front

She realizes she has lived it fully, courageously, has given life and had it taken away. The storm in her heart subsides. The porter comes for her bags. It's a quarter to twelve.

Climbing into her cab, she tells the doorman a young man will call for her a little after midnight. He will be quite excited, insistent. Will the doorman give him a message? Tell him she'll never forget him—will always love him in a very special way. And tell him she's being married tonight! She gives the cab driver orders, "St. Timothy's Hospital, please"... and before the doorman can recover from his bewilderment, she is gone.

There has been a change going on in Ginger's personality. You won't notice it in the picture, because her *Kitty Foyle* will have all the fire and spunk of the modern big city working girl. Privately however, Ginger has become withdrawn and quiet, she will have no part of Hollywood's communal life. On the set, she didn't bother much with the others. When she wasn't actually working in a scene, she retired to her dressing room and played one of the many symphony records she has stacked up beside her portable phonograph.

This is not as unfriendly a gesture as it may seem at first. For one thing, Ginger is in every scene, and the demands of her role are tremendous. When she has a free moment, it is only natural that she use it to store up on energy and catch up on learning new lines. All that, coupled with her newly-acquired r e t i c e n c e, made Ginger somewhat of a stranger to her fellow-workers, in spite of the fact that she reported on the set every day.

But one day, Ginger broke down and perpetrated one of her famous practical jokes. When David Hempstead, the producer of *Kitty Foyle*, celebrated his birthday on the set, he received several wires, at half-hour intervals, which almost broke him up.

"Thanks for trying *Little Miss Broadway*. It did.

"Shirley"

"None of us has worked since then. 'It Could Happen to You.'

"The Down and Out Club"

"*Happy Landing.* They say it's all in knowing how to fall and where.

"Sonja"

"Thanks for *Straight, Place and Show.* We didn't.

"The Ritz Brothers"

When Hempstead asked Ginger if she was the mastermind behind the telegrams, she looked up at him naively and lisped, "Who, me? Oh, Mithter Hempthead, how could you?"

Dennis Morgan was a little nervous doing his first love scene with Ginger. He knows that this picture will be his "open sesame" to stardom, and the thought gave him the jitters. The set was *Kitty's* tiny apartment in New York. *Wyn* has surprised her with a visit, and there is a thrilling reunion.

Hollywood's Strangest Romance

By ANN DAGGETT

■ Orson Welles, the boy wonder of cinema-land, was lonely! He had been for some time, despite the nicest, fattest, juiciest contract that any movie studio had ever handed a newcomer. He had freedom to write, direct and act in a movie. He had fulfilled his life-long ambition. Magazine writers were flocking to write stories about his genius, for he was only 24 years old and wore a beard. He was living in a 14-room house with a swimming pool (also a life-long ambition). But he lived there with his press agent, Herb Drake, who tells how they used to wander through their mansion, each occupying a different bed each night so that the servants wouldn't know that they never had any guests. Orson Welles was marvelous "copy" for the local reporters, but he was the loneliest human being alive. He had been in Hollywood two months and he didn't know a soul.

Then came an invitation from Ann and Jack Warner to attend a party at their home. Orson spent days, literally, wondering about those he would meet.

Music was playing softly as Orson arrived —alone. As he entered the room, the gay conversation came to an abrupt stop and everyone in the room turned to stare at the 24-year-old boy who was such a sensation. Orson's gaze found a pair of laughing black eyes that belonged to the loveliest girl he had ever seen. He stood still for a moment, let his gaze drink in the haze of faces, then looked back at the girl with the haunting black eyes. Jack Warner, sensing the magnetism these two held for each other, steered Orson straight to Dolores del Rio's side. There were introductions and then Dolores talked for a few moments and was gone.

"I was terrified," Orson laughed. "I had never met the beautiful Dolores del Rio and it was a sensation out of this world."

Shortly after the Warners' party, Orson began long stretches of work on *Heart of Darkness*. There was no time for play. There were scripts to be written, sets to be designed, preliminary work to be considered. Months passed and then *Heart of Darkness* was abandoned and a snap decision to make a thriller-melodrama sent him skyrocketing into action on *Smiler With a Knife*. R-K-O refused to give official sanction to the script and then work on *Citizen Kane* began.

During all this time Orson's meeting with Dolores was constantly in his thoughts—but he couldn't contrive any way of meeting her again! This brainy giant who had stunned the world with his brilliance, never even thought of the telephone until many many weeks of needless anxiety had passed. He finally called.

Across the dinner table Orson found himself intrigued by the idea of one who had nerve enough to order a gardenia salad—a favorite dish of the exotic Dolores! Dolores in turn found herself watching Orson eat a four-inch thick steak—his favorite dish. Like two school children they giggled over each other's taste in food.

Came days in Palm Springs when they basked in the warm glow of the California sun. Days fishing off Santa Catalina Island and days spent painting in the open air. There was a quietness and reserve about Dolores

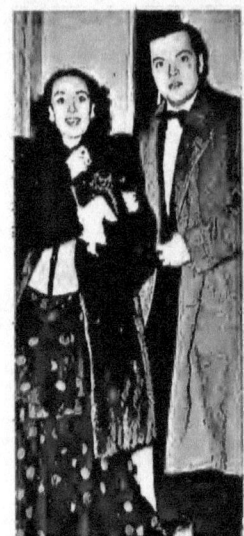

Although many years his senior, Dolores del Rio has proven herself the perfect companion for Orson Welles. He declares they will marry when her divorce is final

that allowed for understanding of this boy genius whose personality was secretly envied by all but openly acknowledged by a mere handful.

Asked whether they would marry, Orson replied emphatically, "I'm going to marry Dolores del Rio and I don't care who knows it. Tell the whole world if you like."

Orson knows he is defying public opinion in announcing his coming marriage to Dolores at this time.

"We know it is improper and rather indecent, to say the least, for us to become engaged before Dolores' divorce is final," Orson explained pointedly. "But what could we do?

"Newspaper photographers were hounding us. The press demanded statements. The private sanctity of our homes was being violated. We have nothing to hide. We are just two people in love. As soon as all this is over, we are going to be married. The wedding will be as inconspicuous as possible and we hope that from then on we can live our lives as ordinary people do."

There is a curious story behind this strange romance of Orson Welles and Dolores del Rio. Orson regards Dolores as a queen and he plans some day to make a picture which will shower her with public favor. Dolores regards Orson much as a mother would a bright and charming child. Orson is still a little boy who likes to play with electric trains, dotes on puppet shows and likes more than anything else to have a sympathetic audience for his magic tricks.

With her understanding heart, Dolores, although many years his senior, enters completely into the spirit of play with Orson. It was she who gave him bean bags at Christmas time and then became so skillful at the game herself, that she was able to beat the entire Mercury Players' staff. However, for all his child's play, there is still a curious contradiction here, for Orson is also a mental giant whose working days are 40 or 50 hours long and whose waking hours are spent writing, directing or acting until the people who can keep pace with him gradually drop out from sheer exhaustion. This may all come under the heading of genius, but it's difficult to live with.

Orson is the first to admit that he can be at fault. He has been married once. His first wife was Virginia Nicolson, whom he met during a theater festival in Woodstock, Illinois. Miss Nicolson's father and Orson's guardian both opposed the marriage bitterly—Orson was only 19, and his bride just a mere 18. The older people were right. The marriage was a failure. A divorce was granted two years ago.

Both Orson and Dolores know some of the pitfalls of marriage and the heartaches that come from mismating. Both are determined that nothing will spoil this marriage.

"I'm confident that we will make a success of our marriage because we are good companions. We understand each other. We like to do the same things. We both like to paint. I've always wanted to be a painter," Orson confided wistfully, "and perhaps some day I shall. Writing takes brains, directing takes nervous energy, and acting takes animal vitality—but painting, well, you just paint."

The real test of their relationship came when *Citizen Kane* was about to be barred from release. There was scandal and intrigue and bitter things said about him. Attacks were leveled at him daily in the press—attacks which he was unable to answer because no avenue of publicity was open to him. Perhaps *Citizen Kane*, the pride and joy of Orson's life would never be shown on the screen. No one will know just what Dolores' kindness and understanding meant to Orson Welles during this period. Her belief in him made him fight for his rights. Although Dolores was in the background as far as the public was concerned, she was by his side, fighting with him a battle which he must, and finally did, win.

It was a proud Dolores who took Orson's arm and shared the spotlight with him at the triumphant opening of *Citizen Kane*. They had fought a battle together and won. ■

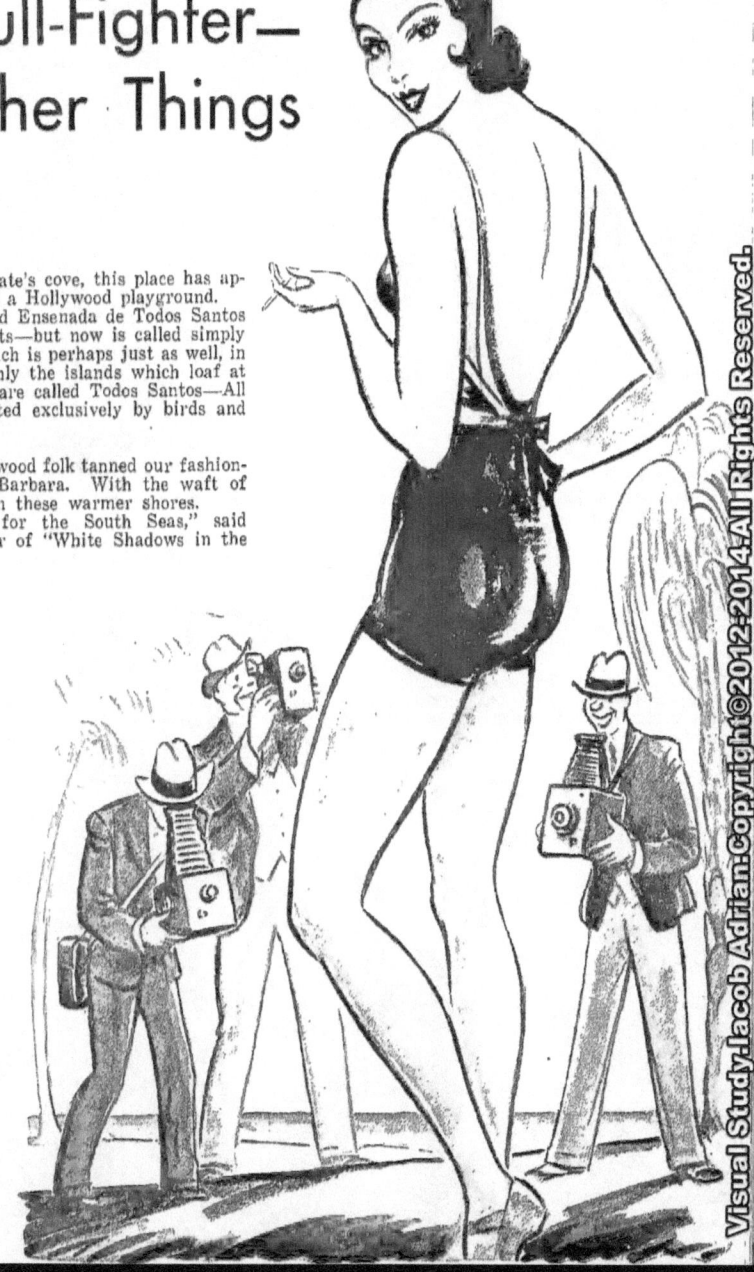

By HERB HOWE

THE BOULEVARDIER

Turns Bull-Fighter—
and Other Things

Ensenada, Mexico:

ORIGINALLY, a pirate's cove, this place has appropriately become a Hollywood playground.

It was christened Ensenada de Todos Santos —Bay of All Saints—but now is called simply Ensenada, or the Bay, which is perhaps just as well, in view of developments. Only the islands which loaf at the mouth of the harbor are called Todos Santos—All Saints. They are inhabited exclusively by birds and seals.

LAST Summer, we Hollywood folk tanned our fashionable hides at Santa Barbara. With the waft of Winter, we are nuding on these warmer shores.

"The best substitute for the South Seas," said Frederick O'Brien, author of "White Shadows in the South Seas."

"Three hours by motor car from San Diego, Ensenada has an ocean beach finer than any other on the Pacific Coast," he said. "A magnificent *concha* of glittering silver sand, seven miles in curve, unmarked by man."

Since Mr. O'Brien wrote those lines, there have been plenty of markings. You can hardly comb the beach for bodies. Still, if you don't mind walking a mile or two up the beach, it is possible to get an all-over tan, like

It was here that the modest Dolores was first persuaded to be photographed in a bathing suit.

DRAWINGS BY
CHAMBERLAIN

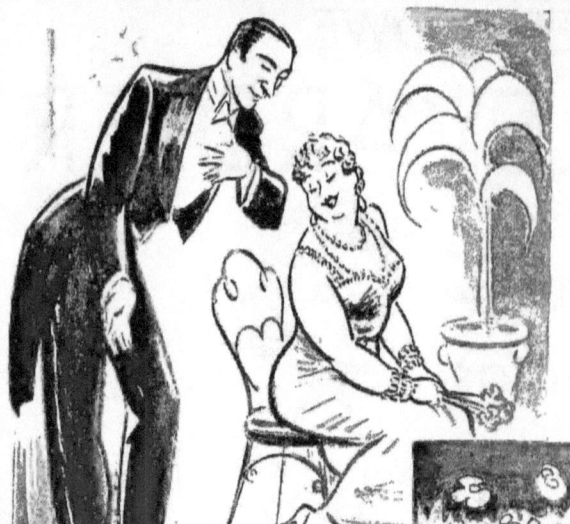

breakfast room with delicately grilled windows gazing seaward, flower-scrolled patios where you may lunch in bathing suit to the lascivious Marimba, a labyrinth of corridors and turret stairs illumined by the murals of Martinez.

As you come around the turn in the bay and behold this dazzling structure roofed in rose with Moorish domes and towers and palmy terraces enthroned on a wild, naked beach, against a background of raw brown mountains, the effect is that of a shimmering mirage.

This is not a solitary rave. Bing Crosby on beholding the place when he came here for deep-sea fishing, just naturally burst into "Paradise," and all the lady fishes went for him hook, line and sinker.

ENSENADA is still going for hermiting. It's not as accessible as the other Hollywood resorts—Palm Springs, Del Monte,

A brilliantined knight-in-tails raises her hand gracefully to his lips.

Peter, the Hermit, used to be *the* hermit in Hollywood—now he has so many rivals he has become very bitter.

Garbo, on the warm bosoms of protective sand dunes. Ensenada is the ideal spot for going native luxuriously.

A SPANISH palace has arisen on the *concha* which magnificently surpasses any hotel of our American shores. It has a dining room suggesting the House of Parliament, a domed casino, two voluptuous bars, a

Santa Barbara, Agua Caliente, Laguna, Arrowhead. The sixty-five mile border is picturesque, but twisty and unpaved.

One should come by plane or yacht. This appeals to the exclusives, such as Garbo and Barrymore and Boulevardier. Yet, many are willing to motor for the sake of the pleasures denied them under the stars and stripes.

The Mexican bell-boys,

The gang society is a bore. So it is most places!

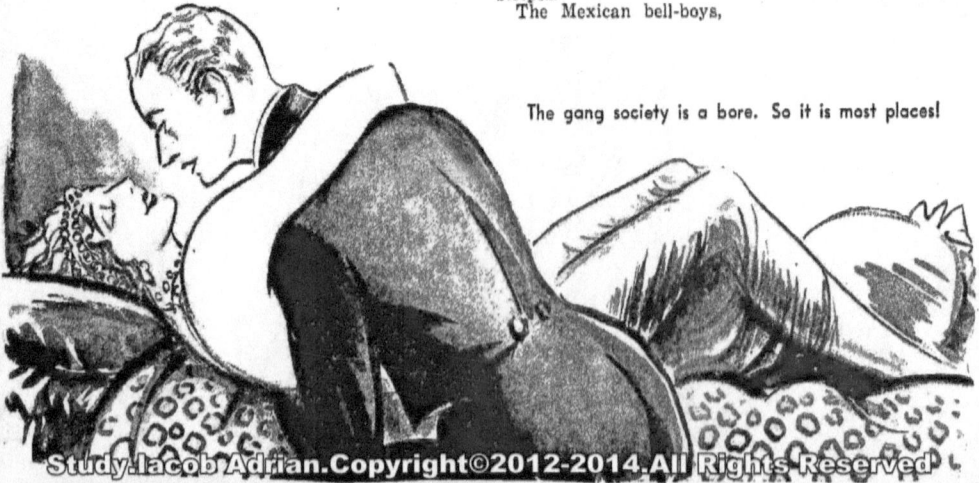

The Boulevardier Turns Bull-Fighter

suggesting robins in their red-breasted coats, have a bell system to announce the type of cars arriving.

If it is a Ford or Chevrolet, they ring once; for the Buick and cars of that order, they ring twice; de luxe cars, call for three pressures.

If I ever drive down in my Rolls, I shall expect the band to strike up.

THE Plaza Ensenada Hotel scorns the common sports of American places, such as golf and tennis and polo. It features those which you cannot enjoy above the border. For the past two weeks, I've been catching up on my beach-combing and bull-fighting.

The Plaza de Toros is in back of the hotel. There is a bull-fight every Sunday. Anyone may enter as a torero. An Italian count was in charge of the bull pen last Sunday, and I recognized my waiter among the bull-fighters; also the troubadour who sings to a guitar in a gentle voice each evening at the bars.

After the first combat, I decided to enter the ring. The first bull was shy and blinked dazedly at the crowd and the band. When he recognized the movie stars in the grandstand, he nearly fainted with embarrassment and rushed back to the pen.

The second bull wasn't interested in anybody. He seemed to be anemic and suffering with world-weariness. He just yawned at the prancing toreros. Instead of becoming indignant when a red blanket was brandished, he looked as though he would like to curl up in it. By that time, I was feeling the same way and so ambled back to the rear for a tanning siesta.

I know I'm going to like bull-fighting; it's so restful.

Dolores Del Rio yachted into the harbor with a party. Dolores owes a lot to Ensenada. Rather, America does. It was here that the modest Dolores was first persuaded to be photographed in a bathing suit. If you saw her in "The Bird of Paradise," you will appreciate Ensenada's contribution to art.

HOLLYWOOD is a gilded cage from which the birdies fly the minute they've tweeted off a picture. Dick Barthelmess goes bounding to China or Russia or Greenland.

Will Rogers flies off in all directions. Dietrich has a contract that gives her six months in Europe. Garbo has arranged for similar vacations. Warner Oland goes to his farm in Massachusetts or to Europe.

Raymond Hatton and Wally Beery lam for the High Sierras. Janet Gaynor has a house in Honolulu. Doug Fairbanks can't stay home long enough to make a picture any more; he takes a camera along and shoots en route. He's even got quiet Harold Lloyd to vagabonding with him.

Yet Hollywood is the cynosure of the world, the paradise of earthly Mahomets. Perhaps that's the trouble. Food's too rich. You get fed up on it.

PETER, the hermit, used to be *the* hermit in Hollywood; now he has so many rivals he is bitter. Garbo, the hermit, has put him quite out of the picture. It's fashionable to recluse.

When Ronald Colman finishes work he evaporates. Ramon Novarro disap-

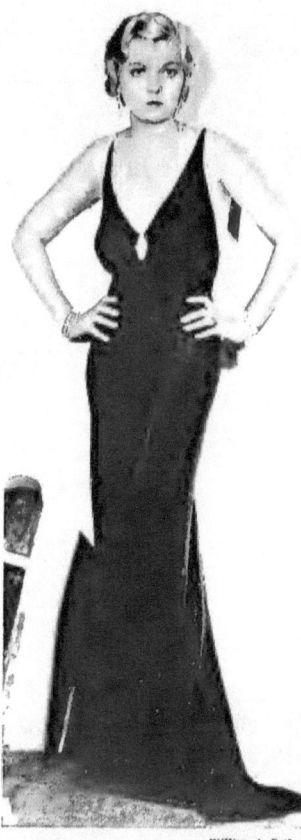

William A. Fraker

Mayo Methot plays an important part in "The Night Club Lady." The black and white satin evening gown is an original creation by Irene Jones. She will next be seen in Columbia's "Virtue" and "Vanity Street."

pears in San Francisco. Even Joel McCrea—current queens' favorite—grows a beard, cooks his own coffee and sleeps in a tent up the beach alone.

I'm not one to speak sarcastically of this Getting Away From It All. For years I've been circling around Hollywood like a crow, swooping down, then taking off to beach or crag.

Pola Negri said, "Hollywood is bluff, bluff, all bluff." It seems even actors get tired sometimes of pretending. So you can judge how tired the rest of us must get pretending to be interested in the pretending.

THE most satisfying way to account for this Hollywood truancy would be to ascribe it to that divine restlessness of genius. Each, interviewed personally, would probably agree to that.

At the same time each would speak of the pretense, the lack of sincerity, the hypocritical back-slapping—on the part of the others.

Those who are not actors will tell you that all actors are insufferable bores. Those who are actors will privately agree that this is true—with notable exception. I don't agree with either. At any rate I would add an "s" to exception. Ramon Novarro is the best one-man show I know and never a bore.

Warner Oland, who never acts off-screen, is the most charming, regaling of companions, with never a display of egotism. Everyone who travels with Doug Fairbanks has a great time and hangs with him for years. Harold Lloyd is so self-effacing as a host that my old army pal, Joe Reddy, the Lloyd publicity man, orders Harold around to pour drinks . . . Harold himself never drinking.

TRUE the gang society is a bore. So is it most places. And you miss the permanent friendship of other towns. Everyone in Hollywood is transient. There's a complete revolution every few years. But there's one point never touched upon in explaining Hollywood's restlessness.

The climate. It's sultry, enervating, tedious, a reclaimed desert that would be ideal for lizards. Understand, I'm not reflecting on the habits of lizards. My tendency is to emulate them. But these gringoes who have taken possession won't let you.

You must work. And because politics figure in studio success, social duties are part of the work. Somerset Maugham once asked me how anyone could work in this semi-tropical atmosphere.

I referred him to his work in the South Seas. He said he didn't work there—just made notes and did his writing when he returned to Paris. Anyhow, he said, one did not have conventional obligations in South Sea Islands—no dressing no premieres to attend, nothing much to do but fan the body by day and dispose of it as one pleases in the scented moonlight.

Having spoken thus of the Hollywood climate I expect to become a permanent hermit—with best wishes of the Chamber of Commerce.

WE'RE fed up on Easterners coming to Hollywood telling us we don't know what the depression is. At first we took this as a compliment to our acting. You know how we laugh clown though the heart is broken.

But we soon realized we were too good. These big barnstormers from the East were grabbing all the sympathy. "Look," they screamed, "We've lost everything and yet we laugh!" Whereupon they gave an imitation of laughter that on sound film would register as the dying screech of a wrung hen.

Eastern papers have been filled with sob stories about brave New Yorkers who, unable to open their houses at Palm Beach this Winter, have bravely gene to Majorca to loaf. Chicagoans are just as drippy. All their papers wept for the proud family who lost *everything* and is now courageously living abroad on eighteen thousand a year.

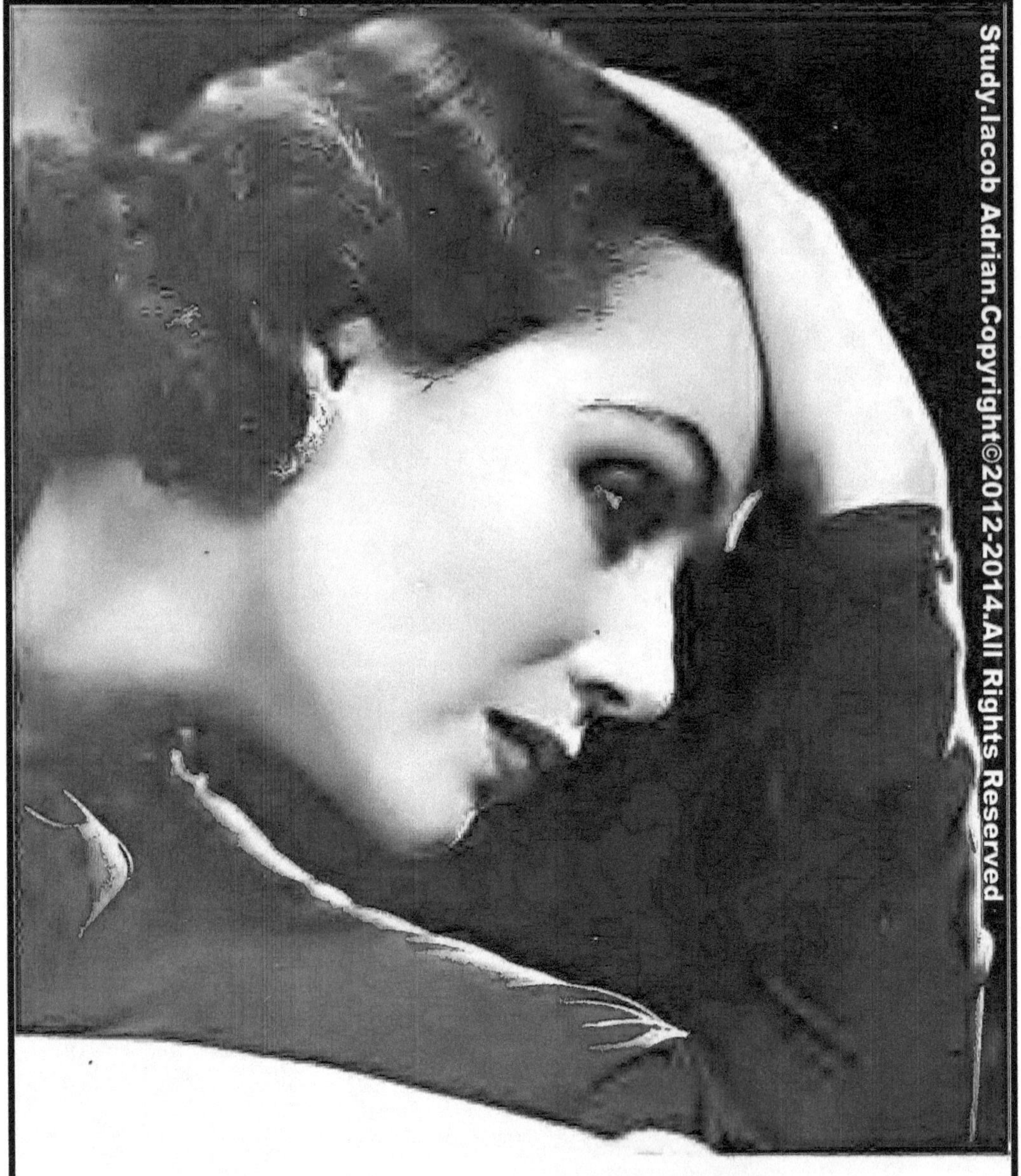

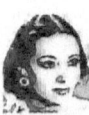

DOLORES DEL RIO—Senora of true Latin loveliness. Daughter of Mexico's distinguished banker, Jesus Asunsolo. She was educated in Mexico City, Paris and Spain, specializing in music and terpsichory. Her charm and grace attracted movie director on location in Mexico some years back. She yielded to Hollywood offer. And fans throughout the world appreciated her glamorous talents until her temporary retirement after her marriage a couple of years back to Art Director Cedric Gibbons. Now she has returned to the cinema swing. "Flying Down to Rio" displays her varied talents. The Gibbons menage is smartly modernistic. Dolores loves clothes, sun baths and Cedric. And of course her work.

"I had always adored dancing, but it would fatigue me. I loved sports but could' take part in none. I found myself sinking lower and lower," says Dolores Del Rio as she bares her private life for New Movie Readers.

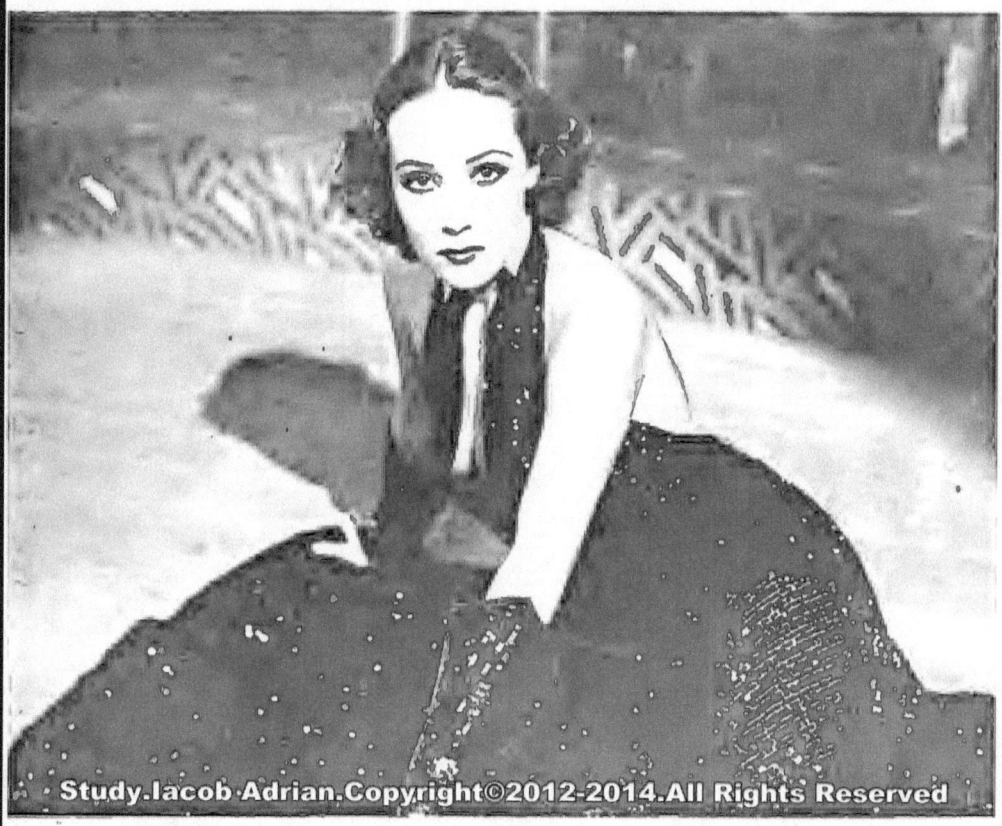

Exotic Dolores

By IRENE THIRER

THE interviewer sank into the downy divan in the Del Rio drawing-room, and actually turned down a highball proffered by the exotic, smart Dolores.

Smart! That's how Dolores Del Rio strikes you immediately. Smart, well-poised, charming of manner. Her voice is softly modulated, with the merest trace of Latin accent.

One isn't surprised to learn that she completed her education in the finishing schools of Spain and Paris; that her father, Jesus Asunsolo, president of the bank of Durango, Mexico, sent her abroad to study painting, sculpturing, dancing, piano and singing.

Her mother—and the two are still inseparable—chaperoned her and encouraged her, especially in the matter of vocal training. And Dolores, familiar with all the arts, would rather dance than sing or paint or play the piano.

She is an actress, and as such has full chance to display dramatic outbursts such as no ordinary mortal can get away with—but she doesn't. Nobody ever hears Dolores raise her speaking tones unless she's on the set and her part requires a flare of temper.

Then, at the director's word, her bright eyes flash, her white teeth gleam between parted red lips, the nostrils of her perfectly chiseled nose dilate in tempestuous fashion.

"I do not say that I take the screen as seriously as I did in 1926, right after I was named a Wampas star," Dolores declared to me. "For six years, I lived for my work alone. I enjoyed no private life. I gave up whatever domestic happiness I had for a career.

"And it was amazing how great a hold the movie studios managed to get on one, considering that it took months of persuasion before I finally consented to accept a screen test.

Exotic Dolores

Exotic Dolores

Exotic Dolores

I am sure there are hundreds of girls as capable as I who can get nowhere near a studio.

"It seems as though I wasn't grateful for my opportunity. And I wasn't. But from the moment I visited the projection room and saw the 'rushes' on my first 'bit' with Dorothy Mackaill in 'Joanna,' I felt a great desire to become a film star. I looked at myself and realized how much I had to learn.

"For six years I gave myself over completely; neglecting home duties, endangering my health in my very enthusiasm, making one picture after another, always hoping for praise and endeavoring to take advantage of helpful criticism. I loved every nook of every studio in which I worked.

"I got tremendous satisfaction out of every role I played—even if the picture was poor—because I managed to make myself believe the part.

When my health broke down, nearly two years ago, my physicians warned me not to take my career too seriously. My bedroom substituted for a studio set, and as the months went by I actually learned to like to relax. I never had done so before.

"From school, I entered the social world and was having a hectic swing at it when Director Edwin Carewe won me over to the movies. So my life remained active and emotional to intensity—what with the tragedy which entered (the death of Miss Del Rio's first husband, Jaime Del Rio, Mexican writer whose name she still uses for screen purposes) my screen work, and constant other difficulties. Energy was gradually sapped from me.

"I had always adored dancing, but it got so that the slightest attempt at it would fatigue me. I loved sports, but eventually could partake in none. I found myself sinking lower and lower —even as a conversationalist. I was what we call 'all in.' And I gave in—to the doctors.

"There is nothing like complete rest to revive the spirits, and change the attitude. I relaxed. My wits began to function faster. My limbs grew strong again. From a morose—yes, morose, remorseful figure, I found myself gathering renewed energy, eager for another lease on life—not a hectic one; a sensible, sane, colorful but calm future.

"I fell in love. I married Cedric Gibbons, one of Hollywood's best known art directors. And still I was not ready to return to the films which had learned to dominate me. I felt simply marvelous.

"After a year of domesticity, I felt the urge—but not as it was before. No surging, all-powerful desire to give myself over to the call of the camera. Just a readiness to work, because I was strong again. And a strong, healthy person with an active mind, cannot and will not be idle. Of course I had my home to direct. But I have an excellent service staff. I do not care for bridge games. So I returned to the studios, and took up my career —allowing it to become part of me, but not—as it never will again—all of me!

"I signed with RKO for four pictures. First came 'Bird of Paradise.' 'Flying Down to Rio' was the second, and I loved doing it. Shopping for costumes was a problem—but not nearly the problem I would have allowed it to become in the 'old' days. The girl of the character was sweet, and she had to wear flimsy summer things. We worked on the movie in the early Winter. I couldn't use last summer's clothes because the film won't be released all over the world until next Summer and a movie star just has to set the fashion.

"I couldn't get any of the important stylists to do my clothes because they were at work on spring things and had not yet thought about costumery for next Summer. So I sat down and in one evening designed my own wardrobe—the Del Rio idea of what the well dressed debutante will be wearing in August, 1934.

"It made me awfully happy. I enjoyed tremendously working with the cast—everybody in the picture was sweet. Director Thornton Freeland was patient and clever. But—do you know what intrigued me especially about starring in 'Flying Down to Rio'?"

The interviewer wanted to know.

"Having the dressing-room next door to Katharine Hepburn's. I think she's marvelous. Quite the most interesting personality who has come to the screen since Garbo. She's a vibrant creature; a brilliant actress."

The interviewer asked—"And a charming person?"

Dolores answered—"I don't know. You see, I've never met her. We had adjoining dressing-rooms, but I didn't want to be introduced to her because she's my favorite actress, and I was afraid to have my illusions spoiled. If I don't know her personally, I'll have a belief that she's just as exciting a person as she is in her picture parts.

"But her natural speaking voice is so loud and so dramatic that I couldn't help but hear her conversation. Really, I wasn't ever eavesdropping. In one way I'd like to know her—and then again, I wouldn't. I'll never forget my reactions to Garbo whom I met for the first time last Summer—after having admired her on the screen for years. To me she was the illusive, the exotic, the glamorous, the grand. Then one day Cedric and I were swimming in our outdoor pool which adjoins our tennis courts.

"A young blond girl, wearing a simple sports dress, flat-heeled shoes and bandanna, approached us with a young man and shyly asked if she might use the tennis courts. I said 'Certainly.' Then I realized that I was talking to the great Garbo. She thanked me sweetly, played her game, and before she left she stopped to thank me again. I was tongue-tied.

"I'm a movie fan myself, you know. And here I was face-to-face with my idol. And in my new, cut-out bathing suit I might have looked more exotic than the timid creature who stood beside me—the glamorous Garbo! Since then I have not met Garbo socially, although I understand that she often uses our tennis courts. Cedric knows her well—he designs many of the sets for her pictures, and he thinks she is a nice, sweet, unassuming girl who happens to be a fine actress. Not mysterious, not temperamental. Just shy!

"So, you see, that's why I'd rather not meet Hepburn. My admiration for her histrionics is so sincere. When she returns to the studios after her play has closed, we'll probably be occupying adjoining dressing-rooms again. So perhaps I'll have more to report to you about her on my next visit to New York."

Miss Del Rio's forthcoming RKO production will be "Dance of Desire," written especially for her by Donald Henderson Clarke, widely known novelist who is also a contributor to THE NEW MOVIE MAGAZINE. The actress is delighted with the part, and hopes to "do right by it."

"It traces a dancer's career from her start in the dives of the slums to the time when she is famous in the theatrical world. I feel that if ever I had opportunity to show the result of many years' study, here it is. I will wear many lovely clothes in the picture. I've been on a continuous shopping tour since I've been in New York."

Whereupon, the lady opened for the interviewer's benefit a host of packages. Black chiffons, black crepes, banded with silver, reds, greens, white evening frocks of shiny satin and dull crepes. Gorgeous things.

"I hardly ever wear my personal wardrobe in pictures," Miss Del Rio said, "because what is correct for formal wear and on the street is not photographic material. The camera lends itself to solid colors. And often my personal taste leans toward floral prints and stripes. I have purchased a number of printed evening gowns. I believe they'll be the rage in 1934.

"And when," the curious interviewer wanted to know, "do you intend to take time out to—well to put it bluntly— to have a child?"

Said Mrs. Gibbons: "When I do have a baby or babies, it will not be a matter of 'time out.' A career may be combined blissfully with domestic relations until children come. Then the outside career should be dropped, and babies—until they no longer depend on the mother, should be the mother's sole interest.

"When I am ready to have a baby, I will be willing to give up all else and devote myself to maternity. And since I am not ready to give up the screen and acting, I have no thought at present of having children. I have varied interests and they're quite satisfying. If I have a baby, I'll no longer be content with my other interests. A baby is worth any mother's complete concentration. Isn't it?"

The interviewer who has two children, a capable nurse, and a job, didn't agree. But that's not the point!

Dolores Del Rio anticipates giving up her film career when she anticipates a child—that's the point!

"What does Mr. Gibbons think of you as an actress?" the interrogative interviewer inquired.

"Well, strangely enough, he thinks I'm good. But we rarely discuss our respective work in any professional sense. Of course if I ask for helpful hints, he's happy to offer them. And once in a while I can be of assistance to him. Usually, though, when he leaves his studio and I leave mine, 'shop-talk' is cancelled. We lead the lives of any peaceful, home-loving persons who haven't a thing to do with the world-renowned cinema industry. We're just happy, homey people—and we love it, just as we love one another!" she ended.

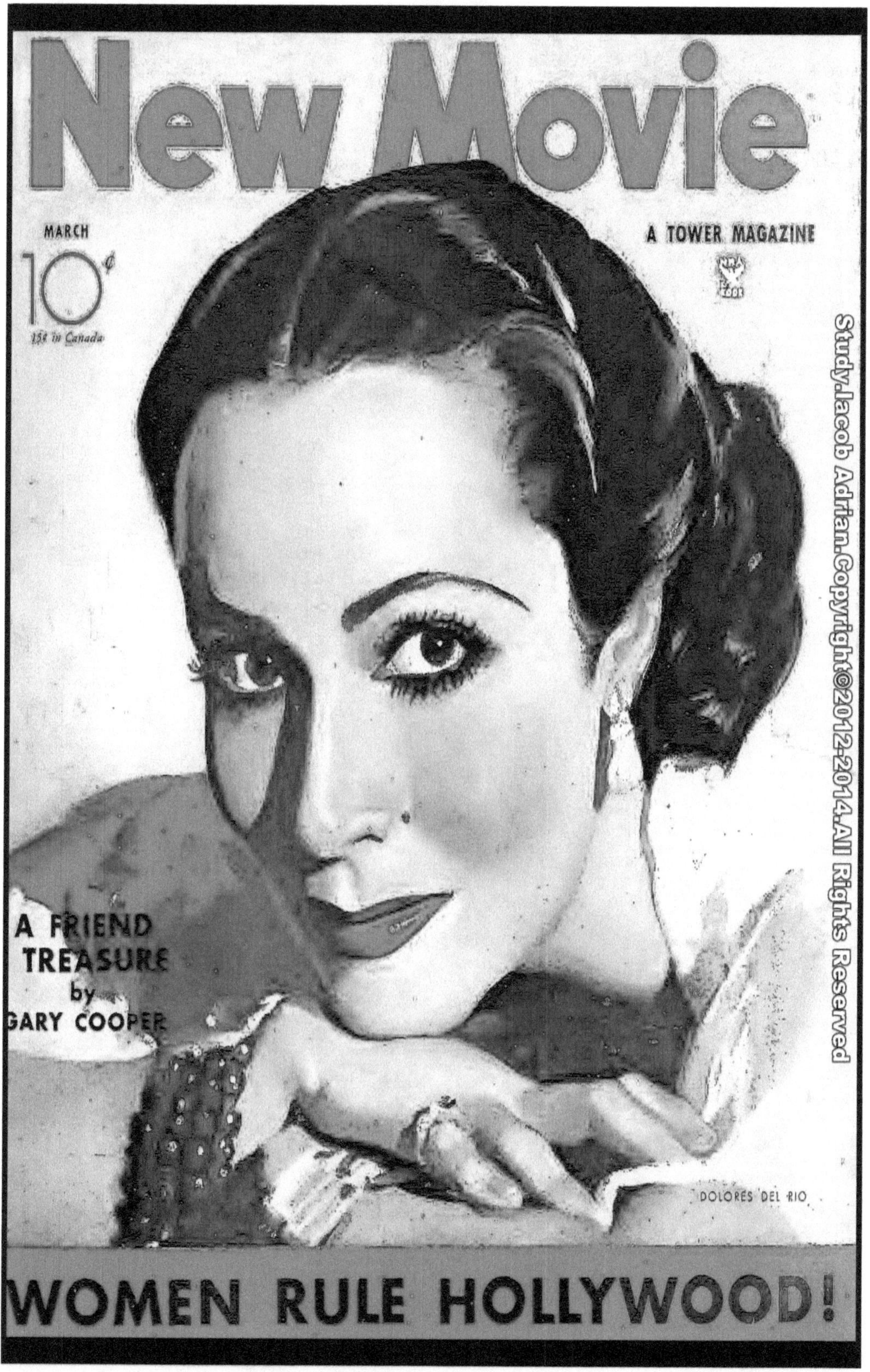

NEW Movie

A TOWER MAGAZINE

MARCH

10¢

15¢ in Canada

**A FRIEND
TREASURE**
by
GARY COOPER

DOLORES DEL RIO

WOMEN RULE HOLLYWOOD!

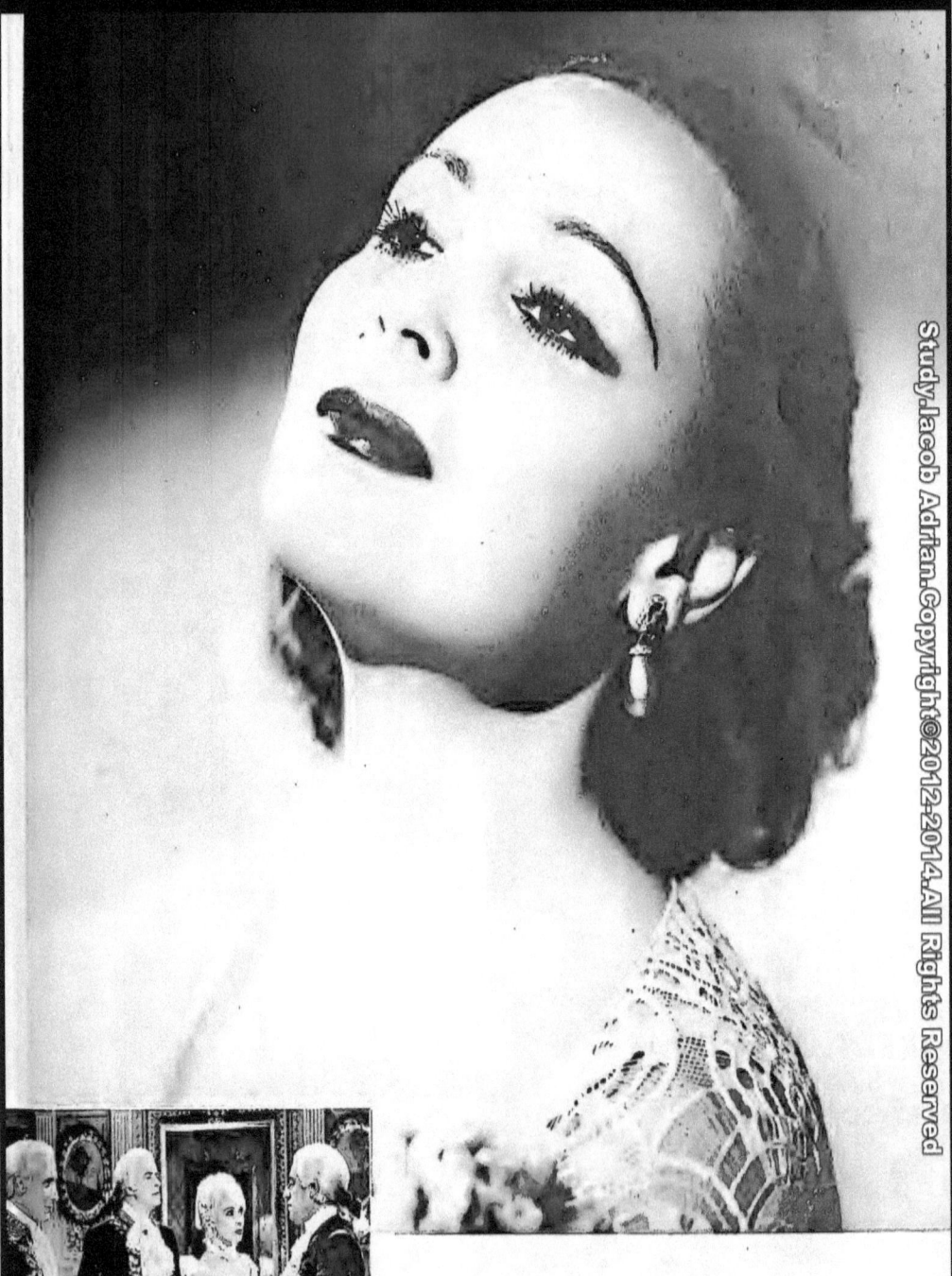

DOLORES DEL RIO

Dolores Del Rio steps from "Madame Du Barry"—there's a scene from it over at the left—into another tempo entirely. "In Caliente," laid in the famous gambling casino across the Mexican border from California, is especially designed to grant opportunities for her personality, a mixture of fire and ice.

IS CALLING ALL STARS

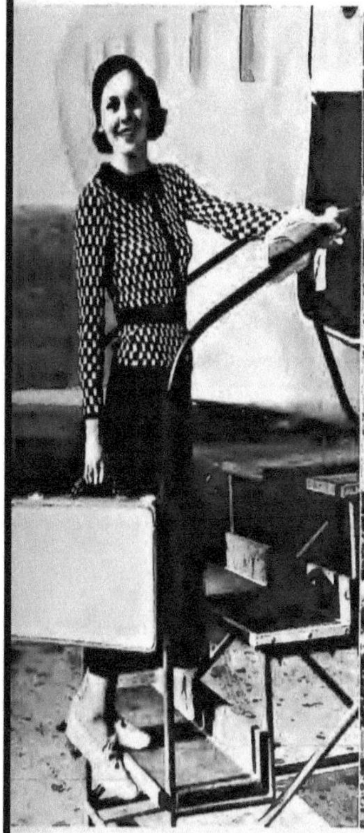

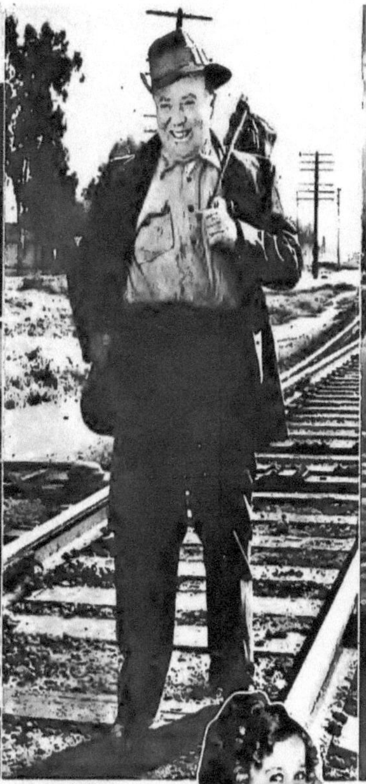

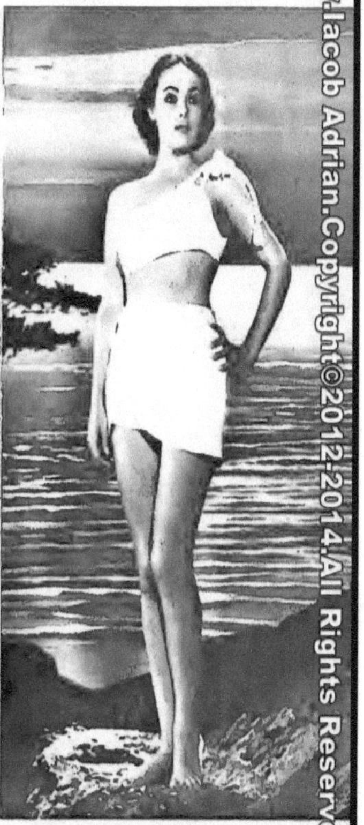

The open road calls in more than one way. Maureen O' Sullivan, for example, takes to wings, while the picture above at the right, shows what Guy Kibbee, in his inner soul, would like to be doing right now.

Above: Dolores Del Rio, with the change of seasons, takes to swimming and the latest thing in *chic* white bathing-suits.

•

But there's no swimming—not yet—for little Shirley Temple. No, for Shirley it's up early and off to school. The boys, below, get a better break. Frankie Thomas can play marbles, any old time of day, with his jockey pal Donnie Meade.

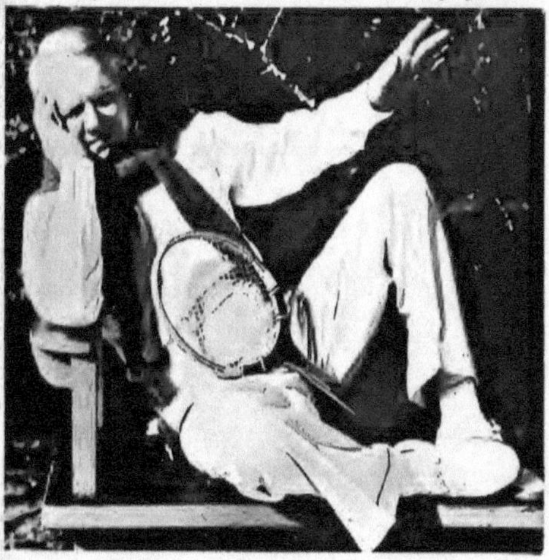

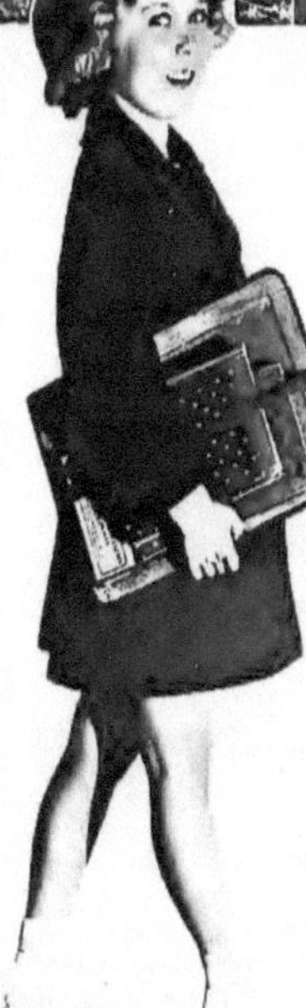

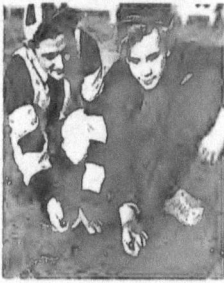

The large picture at the left should erase any last doubts in your mind that Old Winter is gone. Madge Evans is the lovely girl. (Above) "Now is the time for a brisk set of tennis!" says W. C. Fields, promptly toppling over on the bench and into a doze in the sun like an old setter.

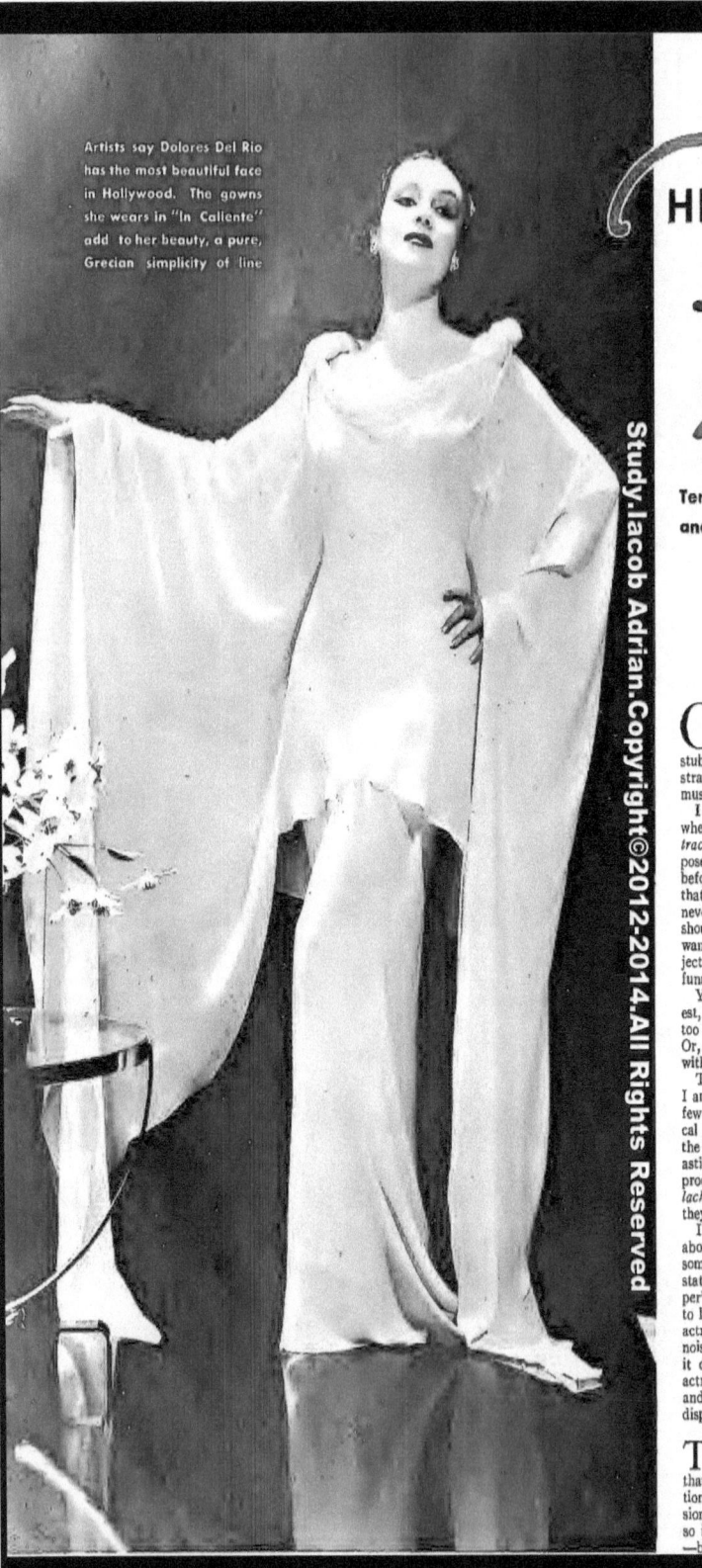

Artists say Dolores Del Rio has the most beautiful face in Hollywood. The gowns she wears in "In Caliente" add to her beauty, a pure, Grecian simplicity of line

HER *four* DEVILS

Temperament, Vanity, Stubbornness and Selfishness. These are the four necessary evils of success

By

DOLORES DEL RIO

OF course I have temperament. Of course I am vain. I am, at times, as set on having my own way as that well-known stubborn mule. And selfish! I am that too. And, strangely enough, these are all traits which one must have to be a success in my profession.

I admit I am guilty of these qualities, because, when they are properly handled, they can be *attractive qualities*. I have developed them all, purposely, since the time I was a small child. And before you say—Yes, an actress can get away with that sort of thing . . . but an ordinary woman, never!—let me tell you that every woman can and should develop a little of these qualities if she wants to become the adored, beloved, spoiled object of some man's affection—as they say in that funny song!

Yes, a woman who is always sweet, always modest, always agreeable and always generous is like too much ripe fruit. You can stand only a taste. Or, another way of saying it, is that a little bitter with the sweet is always appetizing.

Temperament! All actresses have temperament, I am sure, or else they would not be actresses. A few women I know who started out in the theatrical world without temperament, soon found that the theatrical world was not particularly enthusiastic about them. They lacked something, their producers said. They lacked fire. *Because they lacked the ability to stir themselves emotionally,* they lacked the ability to stir others.

I am afraid there is a general misunderstanding about the word *temperament*. Some years ago someone made the rather witty, but incorrect statement that temperament was just plain "temper" without the last syllable. And people began to look upon it as such. When they heard of an actress flaring up on the set and creating an angry, noisy scene, they said, "Ah, temperament!" But it did not occur to them that when that same actress performed a beautiful, sad scene—tender and tearful—that she was also, at that time, too, displaying temperament.

TEMPERAMENT is the blend of many emotional qualities . . . temperament is the thing that enables one to respond, with the same emotional elasticity, to beauty, to ugliness, to depression, to great joy. Just as steel is "tempered," so is a personality made pliable by temperament —both words

Her Four Devils

are derived from the same root.

And temperament is the thing which enables people to express their emotions. That is why, I suppose, that actresses have more temperament than most women . . . because, being actresses, they are constantly exercising their emotions. Most women are self-conscious about expressing their emotions. If they are angry, they try to hide it. If they are enamoured, they also try to hide that. If they feel sympathetic, they try to hold themselves in check. If they are overjoyed they refrain from jumping around the room. I think all this is too bad . . . really I do. An even-tempered, smooth-running personality is like too much of the same color around you. It grows tiresome. A splash of red would perhaps relieve the monotony.

A splash of red in one's personality will attract a man's eye much more quickly and hold it longer than a lovely, even shade of pale pink. (I can always explain things to myself with color analogies, for colors mean much to me.)

LET me tell you a little anecdote to explain it further. There is a young romance which I have been watching for some time. The girl has one of the sweetest dispositions I have ever known . . . always agreeable, always patient, always understanding. The young man, slightly irresponsible, has often taken advantage of this fact . . . breaking dates on occasions, arriving late for appointments, and that sort of thing, all of which she seemed to understand and forgive. Until one day, when she flared up and refused to see him again if he didn't mend his ways. With that little speech she slammed the door in his face. He went away beaming. He was delighted and encouraged. The girl had spirit, after all! Immediately he fell in love with her all over again . . . and he hasn't been known to break a date since.

As for vanity . . . I say *every woman should be vain!* It is one of the most important qualities in an actress . . . and it is only slightly less important in other women. I have been incurably vain ever since I was a little girl. What woman hasn't! In the convent we were taught that vanity was against religion. We were not allowed to wear make-up . . . and even pocket mirrors were denied us. Yet I always managed to have one with me. I made a pocket on the inside of my uniform, and carried one little mirror there. Then, in my desk, on the inside of the top, I tacked a mirror. My mirrors were never discovered, but I *was* punished once for curling my hair. We were all required to wear our hair simply parted in the middle, and hanging in two long braids over our shoulders. One day I stopped my braid half way down the length of my hair, and curled the rest of it. When it was discovered, one of the nuns led me out into a patio where all the girls were gathered for a meeting, and publicly punished me. But it didn't do me any good! The shame of being so publicly punished, even, had no effect on me. My appearance was still of paramount interest.

And so it should be to every woman. Women are entirely too careless about their appearance. They are apt to follow the same beauty routine, month after month, without knowing why. If you ask the average girl why she parts her hair on the side, she is quite likely to say, "Oh, I don't know . . . it just happens to go that way"—when we should never do anything about our looks unless there is a well thought-out reason for it. We must all study ourselves carefully to know which coiffure is the most attractive, which make-up is the most becoming, which style of dress is the most flattering. For one thing, I never allow anyone to see me, even my closest friends unless I am looking my very best, and no woman who respects herself should.

Vanity is something which I think should be instilled in little girls, even as young as ten years old. Not every girl can be beautiful but every woman can be what the French people call *soignee* . . . which means "cared for." And if I can be excused a little pun, I can say that to be *soignee is* to be cared for, by someone. In fact a *soignee* woman is often more attractive than a beautiful one. She is always exquisitely groomed . . . she is neat and spotless and fresh-looking always.

I feel certain that men like vain women. They like to know that a woman takes excellent care of herself, for they know then that, as she grows older, she will never grow any less attractive.

Of course a woman must not be stupid about her vanity. She must not parade it in public places. She must confine her pursuit of beauty to her own boudoir. And if a woman is constantly late because of last-minute primping . . . well, as I said before, that is only stupid, and stupid women never get any place anyway.

My vanity really has two reasons for its existence. There is Cedric, my husband . . . whom I always want to be proud of me. And there are my fans . . . I never want them to see me except at my best. Recently when I flew to Mexico to visit my childhood home there were hundreds of them there at the airport to greet me. And I was greatly criticized for not stepping out of the plane at once to see them, and to let them see me. Yes, I kept them waiting for a few minutes. But that was necessary . . . for in those few minutes I freshened my make-up, combed my hair, and tried to make myself look as attractive as possible. I felt I owed them that . . . and I am sure they were more glad to see me, because of that wait and the way I used that time, than they would have been had I stepped from the plane disheveled and dusty.

As for stubbornness . . . if determination is stubbornness, then I am also stubborn and to a very great degree. To be successful in anything you must fight for what you believe is right, every step of the way. And there are always dozens of people who will do their best to talk you out of anything, particularly if it is something you want very much to do.

Of course there are two kinds of stubbornness . . . stupid, bigoted pig-headedness, and intelligent upholding of a principle. If I am convinced that I am wrong, I can, without any silly pride, swing over to the opposite side and be just as stubborn about it as I was about my former stand. I am quite certain that nobody admires a wishy-washy person who thinks this this moment, and something else the next. But neither is a blindly stubborn person looked up to. Stubbornness is a good quality only when it is intelligent.

The time when my stubbornness came into most importance was when I was fighting to be allowed to do modern parts on the screen, and to get away from always being a native girl. I said that I would not accept another native role, if I had to wait ten years to get the sort of thing I wanted. It was difficult, keeping my promise to myself, but I kept it. I had many attractive scripts submitted to me . . . one from the beautiful book, "Green Mansions" . . . and you can well imagine how strongly I was tempted to do the part of the dream girl in that story. But no! I had sworn that in my next picture I would be a modern girl, wearing modern clothes. That so-called stubbornness kept me off the screen for a year . . . but it was well worth it, for it opened up a new career to me.

As for the last professional trait—selfishness—perhaps you who have tried to be selfish know how difficult it is. I rather think that *selfishness is more of a self-sacrifice than unselfishness*—for unselfishness always reaps a happy reward, even if it is only in the happiness of others, which you, in turn enjoy. But to be selfish . . . it is a thankless job. Yet it is something which every actress should be.

LET me explain. Perhaps this is a bit out of the ordinary, but I honestly feel that I do owe myself to my fans. My producer pays me a salary, only because there are a certain number of you who always go to see my pictures. If I am not always looking and acting my best in my pictures you will not continue to pay money to see me. Therefore I owe to you and my producers and my pictures the best that is in me. To give you that I must be completely selfish. I cannot see my friends while I am working on a picture. I must cancel all my social engagements, and I do not even receive telephone calls. If someone happens to drop in against the rules, at nine, promptly, I excuse myself and say that I must go to bed. It is very rude, I know, but I *must* be rude.

This is not only annoying to my friends—and I promise you, very few of them really understand it—but it also is difficult for Cedric. When I return home from the studio, if my body requires food, I sit down at the table, without waiting for him, and my dinner is served to me. Many times he must eat alone, while I am working, and spend the entire evening alone in the library. Fortunately Cedric, who works in a studio all day himself, understands this form of selfishness, and is tolerant.

I have been criticized on many occasions for refusing to make benefit performances, for declining invitations to talk on the radio, for declining just social invitations. I do not omit these things because I want to, but because I must. I must be selfish, because of my work. It is only good sense. An actress who spreads herself thinly over a number of friends and engagements, gives nothing to any of them. We cannot spread ourselves around or we will have nothing to offer anywhere. We must draw everything, our energy, our spare moments, our inspiration, close around ourselves . . . and *into* ourselves, selfishly, instead of sharing these things with others. It is a rule I had to learn. It did not come naturally or easily. I had to develop the art of being selfish.

But don't you think that because my selfishness, my vanity, my stubbornness and my temperament, even, are devoted to you . . . a gesture for your esteem . . . that perhaps you might forgive me for them? I have a feeling that you will . . . or else I should never have written this story.

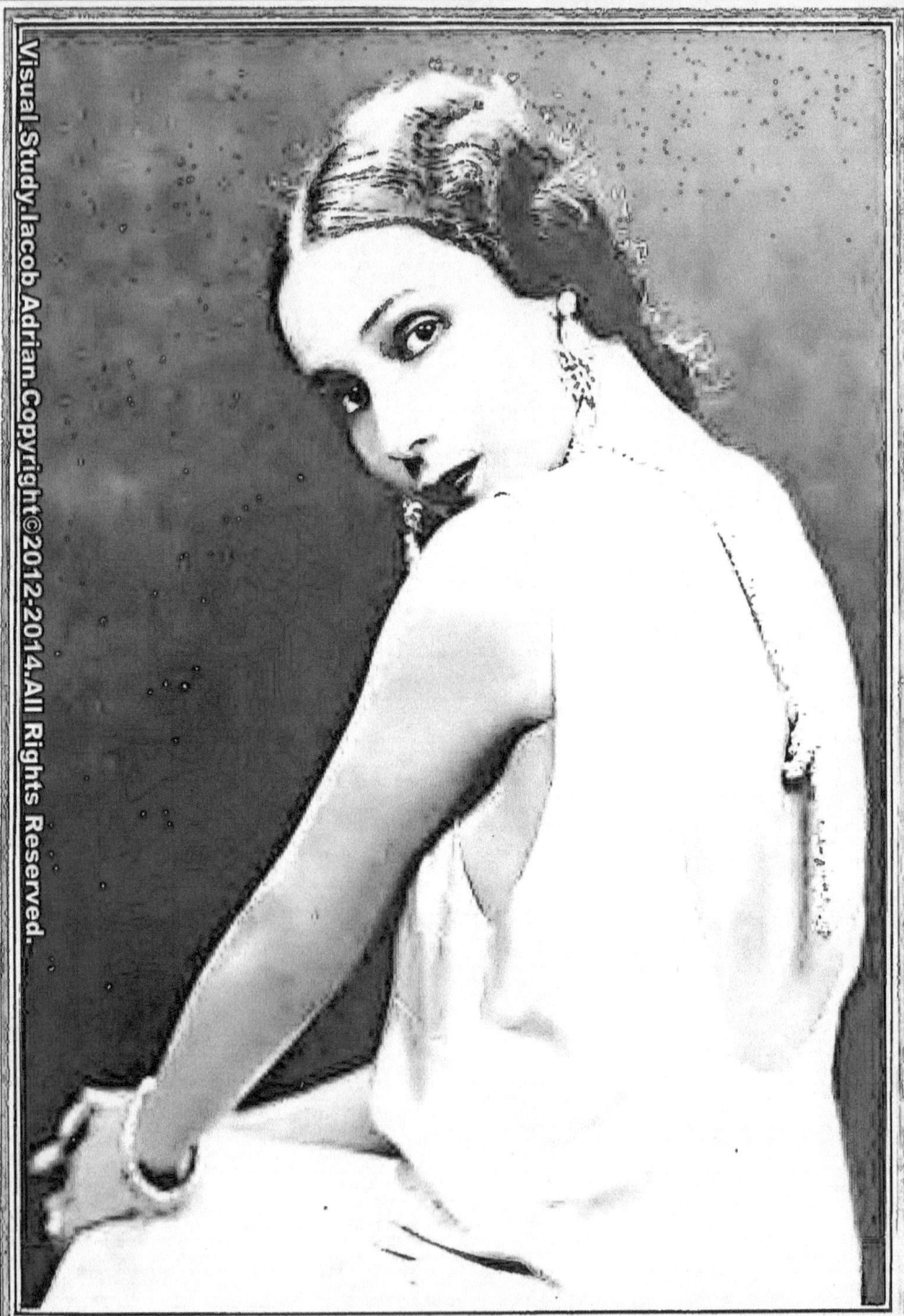

DOLORES DEL RIO

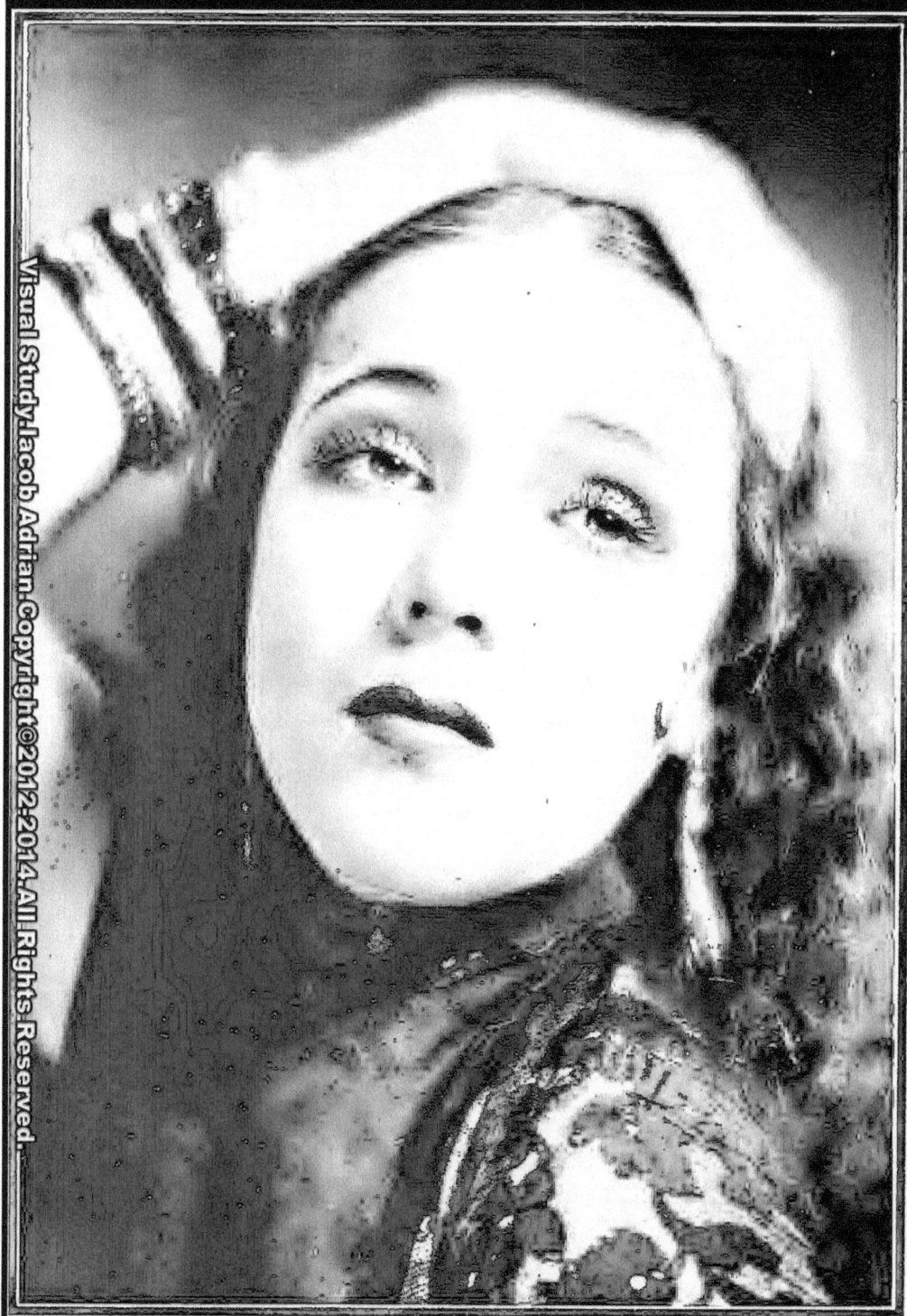

DOLORES DEL RIO

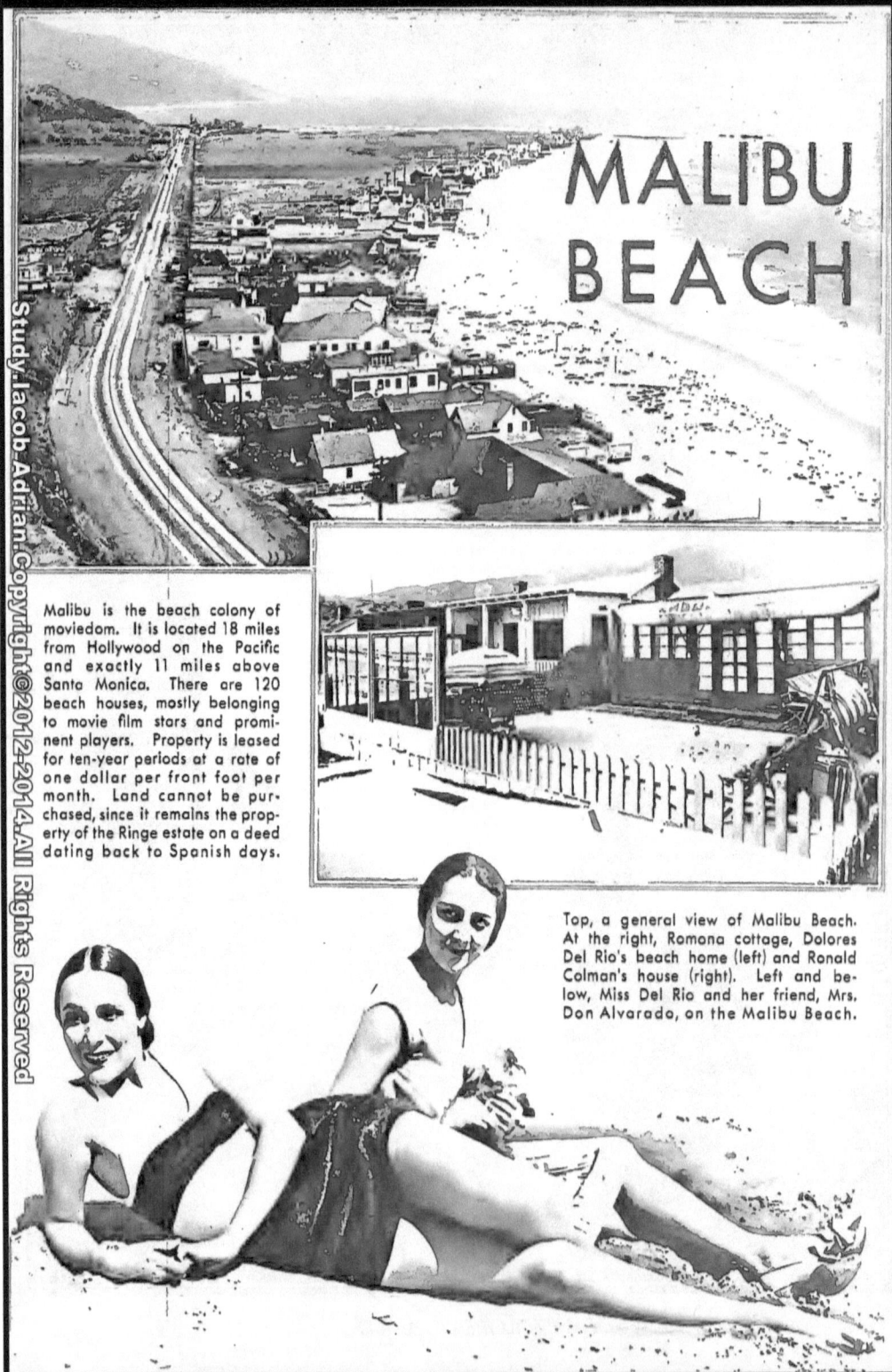

MALIBU BEACH

Malibu is the beach colony of moviedom. It is located 18 miles from Hollywood on the Pacific and exactly 11 miles above Santa Monica. There are 120 beach houses, mostly belonging to movie film stars and prominent players. Property is leased for ten-year periods at a rate of one dollar per front foot per month. Land cannot be purchased, since it remains the property of the Ringe estate on a deed dating back to Spanish days.

Top, a general view of Malibu Beach. At the right, Romona cottage, Dolores Del Rio's beach home (left) and Ronald Colman's house (right). Left and below, Miss Del Rio and her friend, Mrs. Don Alvarado, on the Malibu Beach.

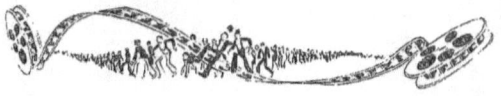

Gossip of the Studios

DOUGLAS FAIRBANKS has gone to England with Leo Diegel and George von Elm to see the international golf matches. Mary Pickford remains at home in Hollywood, to start work on her new talking picture, "Secrets."

As this is the first time since their marriage ten years ago that Doug and Mary have been separated for any length of time, rumors of trouble in the Fairbanks household began to fly as soon as Doug had actually departed.

Both Mary and Doug have treated any such idea with silent contempt. The fact is, probably, that these two famous stars have decided to compromise certain tastes and plans for the future. Mary is wrapped up in her

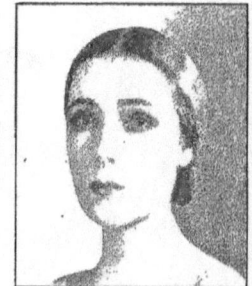

Gary Cooper: "My darling little Gary, I lofe you," says Lupe Velez. The Velez-Cooper romance continues to simmer.

picture work. She is not only making a picture of her own, but anyone who knows anything about it will tell you that Mary Pickford is the chief factor in all of United Artists plans and that she keeps a close eye on both business and production.

Douglas, on the other hand, has lost a lot of his enthusiasm about making pictures. He wants to travel and do many other things. Mary has never cared greatly for a roving life and sporting events don't hold the thrill for her that they do for her athletic husband.

In consequence, this first trip of Doug's without his wife simply indicates that while there is no rift in the domestic happiness, they intend in the future to fulfill their own desires. There isn't anything very unusual about that. Plenty of wives don't trail around after their husbands when they attend polo tournaments and golf matches, and with much less reason for staying home than Mary Pickford has. And many men with as much money and as definite a success behind them as Douglas Fairbanks choose to devote more time to play and less to business.

So there you are. Seems fairly normal. We doubt greatly that anything further will come of it.

* * *

Did you know that Lon Chaney used to sing in Gilbert a n d Sullivan operas? And that his voice will be heard in four parts in his coming picture — his first talkie? You will hear him as an old woman, a ventriloquist, the ventriloquist's dummy, and a parrot.

* * *

COLLEEN MOORE has filed suit for divorce against her husband, John McCormick.

John has sailed for Honolulu and Colleen is living alone in the beautiful home she recently built in Bel-Air. Her mother and one of her closest friends, Julanne Johnson, are visiting her there.

This divorce is the end of a romance that began when Colleen was a little known actress and John McCormick

Dolores Del Rio: Wants good pictures rather than good stellar close-ups. She let Eddie Lowe steal her last film.

was a press agent. Their careers were built together, until Colleen became the biggest box-office attraction among the feminine screen stars and John was head of the First National studios.

Everyone who knows them feels a deep regret over their parting. Colleen intends to go to Europe for some months, unless a highly satisfactory picture contract now in the offing is signed.

Personally, we hope Colleen won't follow her own desire and retire from the screen to travel and study sculpture. We would miss her bright comedy sadly. So far, no one has appeared to take her place.

* * *

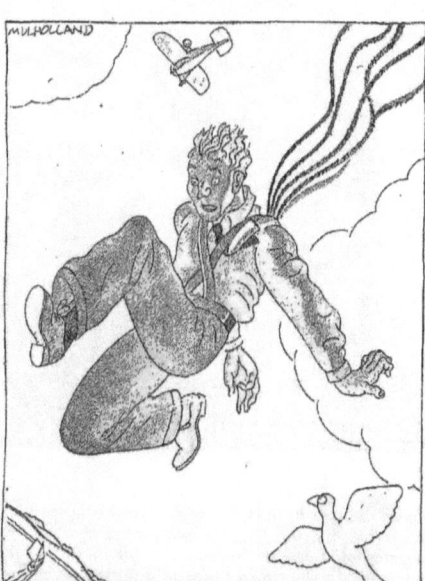

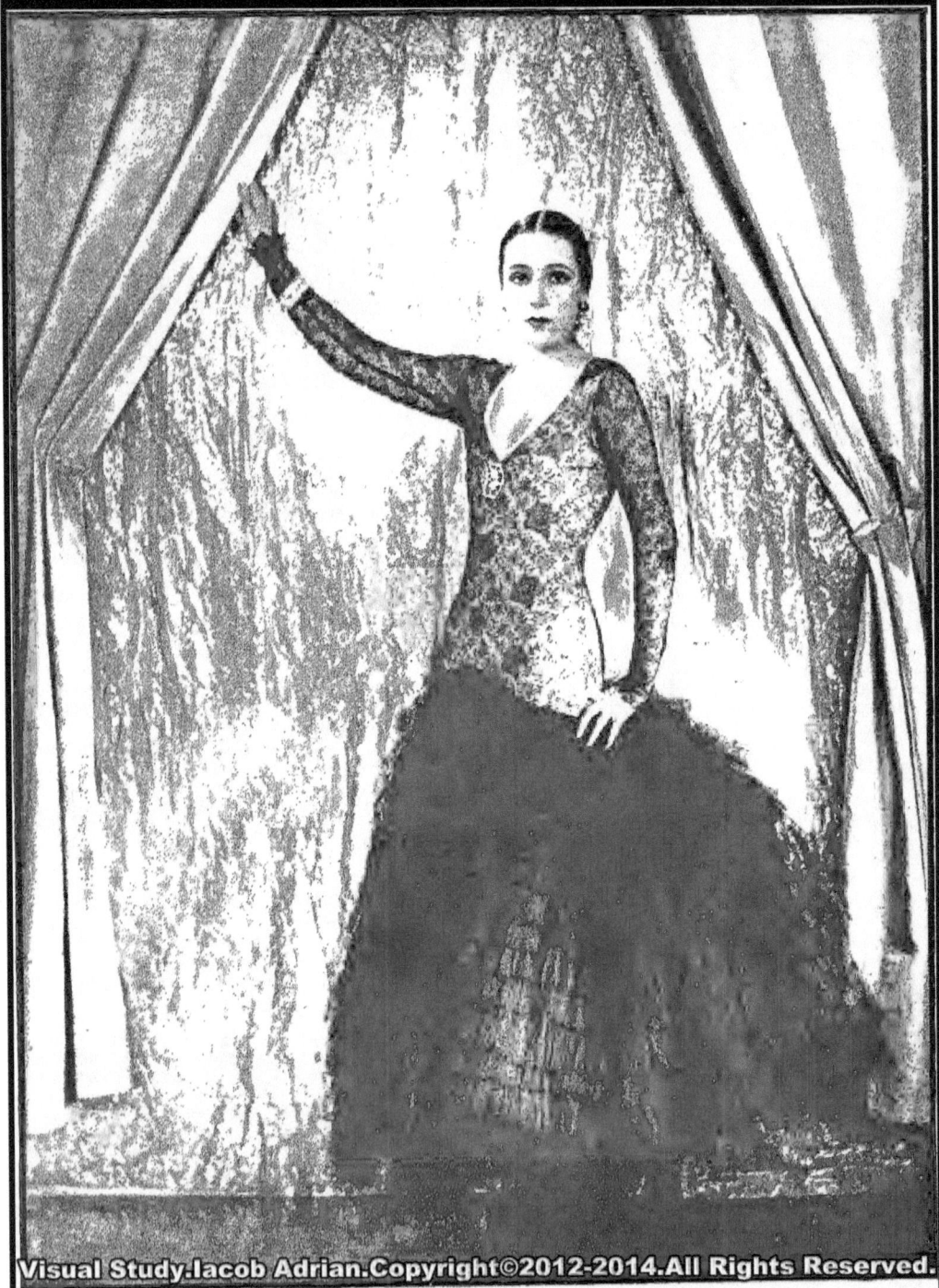

Dolores Del Rio is different from any other girl in Hollywood. Her background, her experience, her education, her philosophy are all different. When she was five, she was placed in a strict Mexican convent. For ten years she lived and moved in the rigid paths laid down by the nuns. At fifteen she left the convent to marry a man older than herself whom she scarcely knew. Finally, when her marriage became unendurable to her she broke away.

"I WANT to be HAPPY"

"For the first time in my life, I am myself," says Dolores Del Rio. "I intend to seek out all the laughter, all the joy, all the amusement."

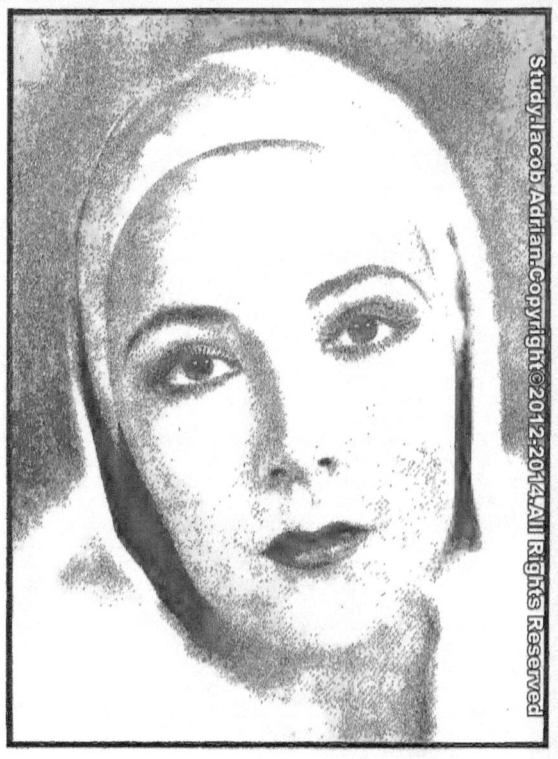

The contrast between Dolores Del Rio's physical appearance and her actual character is surprising. She looks orchidaceous. One imagines her in stately ballrooms, exquisite boudoirs, softly lighted drawing rooms. But that is only one side of Miss Del Rio, the most exploited side, and it is relatively unimportant to her.

BY ADELA ROGERS ST. JOHNS

ANNE ALVARADO, who knows her better than anyone else, says that Dolores Del Rio is the most misunderstood woman in Hollywood.

I rather think she is right.

The hot but heartless Mexican siren suggested by Del Rio's dark beauty vanishes into thin air upon close acquaintance. The luxurious orchid, a lady who loves diamonds and sables and exotic perfumes, presents only one side—and a rather unimportant side—of this lady of quality.

Dolores is different from any other girl now in electric lights. Her background, her experience, her education, her philosophy are all different. Her viewpoint cannot be the same as theirs for these reasons.

When she was five, she was placed in a strict Mexican convent. For ten years she lived and moved in the rigid paths laid down by the most aristocratic nuns.

At fifteen she left the convent to marry a man much older than herself whom she scarcely knew.

Until she was five, Dolores did as her mother said. Until she was fifteen, she obeyed the sisters. After her marriage, she obeyed her husband. She knows what discipline means.

Finally, when her marriage of convenience became unendurable to her, when residence in the United States had convinced her that unhappy marriages need not be borne forever, she broke away, determined to have and do the things she valued and which she had missed.

"Marriage is not for the woman who makes her own living. It is too great a demand." —DOLORES DEL RIO

"AND now, for the first time in my life," she said, "I am myself. I do what I want to do. I get the joy from life. I have the fun I never had when I was a young girl, because so soon I was married—two weeks out of the convent. I have romance, I go to parties, I laugh and talk. All these things most girls have done when they are not yet twenty. Me—I am then the wife to a man much too old, who allows not these things for his wife. Now—I make up for lost time, no? Every person who is human will do so. It is a law of nature. If not one time, then another time.

"But I have been trained, always, to control myself. It is good. Then one does not—run wild, eh? It is possible to stand back and judge of what things are worth, of what is their value to us. It is better.

"For myself, I will be happy all the time, because the world is so full of so many beautiful things. And I make my life, I carve it, with care. Is that not wisdom? I am ambitious for my work. I will do nothing to injure it. But—from life now I get everything I can, every joy, every sensation, all the laughter, all the amusement. Else I starve to death and become an old woman before it is time."

Of Del Rio I would say that she is a woman of charm. The woman of charm must above all things be many-sided in character.

Next, she must be interested in many things and in all people.

There is one thing about Del Rio that is absolutely different from any other motion picture star I have ever

"I Want to Be Happy"

We had started out with a very serious discussion about life. About love. About marriage.

By the time you read this issue of NEW MOVIE Miss Del Rio may be married to Cedric Gibbons. Miss Del Rio had often said that she would never marry again. She qualified that to me. "I have always said to myself that I would marry again only in case I found a man who agrees with my ideas of freedom and progress," she said, moving her small dark hands so that the enormous emeralds glittered. "I have felt that marriage is not for the woman who makes her own living. It is too great a demand. I have believed that marriage of its very self does something to people. Once in love, I realized that I would be like every other woman and expect my marriage to be the one shining exception." Then she met Mr. Gibbons.

Miss Del Rio went on:

"I will show you how marriage affects people. I was married to Jamie Del Rio when I am—just fifteen. Pretty young. I did not know him. I did not love him. I was very, very unhappy. We came to Hollywood, just to travel and make a visit. And for fun, to tell my friends in the City of Mexico, I make a scene. It happened that I looked very nice. So—I make up my mind I would stay and have a career.

"I wanted to do something. Perhaps if my marriage had been happy I would not have wanted it. But I was so miserable. Nobody knew it, for I do not think it is—well bred, so long as you live with a man, to speak ill of him or to discuss your personal affairs. In the end, after much unhappiness, we separate.

"Later, when we are divorced, we met in Paris. And we had a wonderful time. We enjoyed each other every day. We laughed. We were good friends. But when you are married, that seems difficult.

"Do you not think from this—progress we have made, something must be evolved that will solve marriage? This present state is very bad. I, for myself, have been afraid of marriage. More and more women are like that and it is bad. But I believe in progress. We have cast off many things that barred us from full living, from injustice. Now we must learn to adjust freedom to the higher ideals of life. We have overcome fear and stupidity. Now we must build up new and more splendid ideals on that advanced plane we now occupy.

"The mistake is in disregarding all standards, all ideals. That is not only immoral. It is stupid. It leads to boredom—to slovenliness. Bad manners, for instance, merely remove the beauty and delicacy from life. They are senseless.

"I love nice manners. I think I even love a little formality — in its place. Freedom is giving too much of a sameness to life. One loses all the kick. If one behaves the same at an evening party as at a beach picnic, the color and drama are soon gone from both kinds of festivity.

"Yes, I think we are being very stupid. It would be more fun if we were not so loose and so careless."

THEN we got to talking about what a funny party you could give in Hollywood—an "Ex" party. Everyone is writing books about Ex something or other. So we thought an Ex party would be grand. We didn't spare anyone there. We thought it would be in keeping to invite Leatrice and Jack Gilbert and Ina Claire and Gene Markey and Greta Garbo. And we kidded Colleen to death about the party to which she invited Ben Lyon and Bebe Daniels and Jack Pickford and Marilyn Miller.

"That was quite all right," said Dolores. "They are all ladies and gentlemen. I am sure they had fun."

"You see," she said, "the law of life is movement. Life moves. Every seven years our whole body is renewed. Why not the mind? How can one tell what one will be like seven years from now? It may be that certain things are immortal. They will remain seven times seventy. But they will take care of themselves. We must not worry because we change. That is wonderful. Only the dull and the stolid are changeless. Consistency is not always admirable. I do not worry that I change. I am happy. That is life. Now I have a good time. Later, maybe I will not. But—I live."

As we left the table Colleen said: "That is a swell person."

Yes. A woman of charm. A lady of quality. Unconfused, poised, sophisticated, warm toward life but regarding it with steady eyes. Unafraid, but wisely cautious. Well educated, well read, widely traveled, adaptable to any situation. Perfectly at ease always, perfectly natural, disdaining affectation as she disdains dishonesty, but not throwing her knowledge in your face.

The more I think of her, the more I am inclined to heave a long sigh of relief. We can use a lot like her in Hollywood.

The Story of Hollywood's Most Misunderstood Woman

met—with the exception of Marion Davies. Self seems missing from Del Rio's actions and her vocabulary.

IN a land where personality is the chief commodity and where the battle for success is violent and continuous, it is but natural that the majority of people should be self-centered. To some extent they must be. Many are quite frank about it, not a few are actually so interesting that nobody minds, some take it out in an inferiority complex, which is more self-centered than most things. But almost all of them concentrate upon self.

Dolores Del Rio is different. Not from any great unselfishness of character, such as controls Miss Davies, but simply from sureness, from confidence. She knows what she wants. She knows exactly how to get it. She knows what she can do. Therefore, she can afford to ignore it all. She need not be either on the offensive or the defensive. She can be herself—and be charming. Her mind and her time are free for other and broader views.

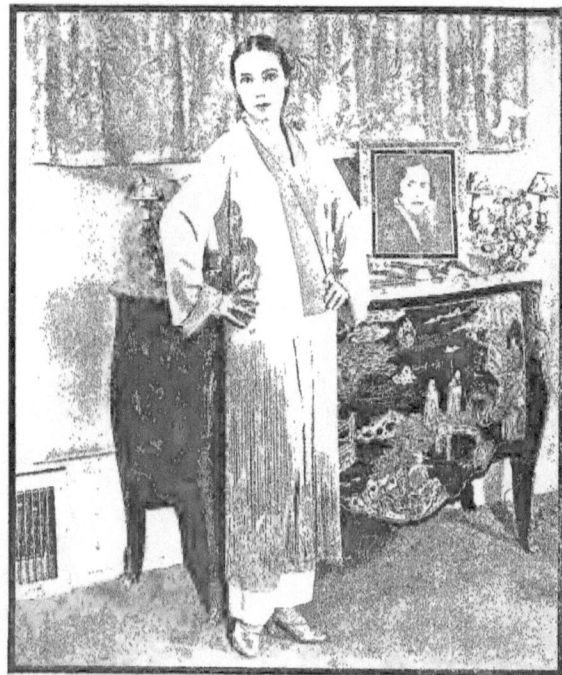

Dolores Del Rio in the Louis XV room of her beautiful Hollywood residence. Standing on the chinoiserie dresser beside her is a portrait of her mother.

The things she loves best are all outdoors.

I have seen her lie for hours on the beach at Malibu, with nothing on but an old, faded bathing suit. The sun and the sand she revels in, doesn't care in the least how she looks. Dripping with sea water, she comes out of the ocean, her hair plastered like black patent leather, and races up and down the beach, as unself-conscious as a child. Often she comes to her beach house alone and spends three or four days in the sun, reading, resting, thinking.

Last year she and her dear friend, Mrs. Don Alvarado, camped for weeks alone in the high Sierras. They did their own cooking, made their own beds, tramped the trails all day and at night sat silent and happy beside their little campfire.

Few women care for the high Sierras, even with plenty of company. They are beautiful, the most beautiful places in the world are in the Sierras near Yosemite, but they are big and lonely. Beneath the purple grandeur of those sky-reaching peaks, among the majestic, wise old trees, beside the murmured, age-less poetry of the winds and the splendid waterfalls, the human soul faces something of eternity and all there is of immensity.

I have known many, many people to run away from those mountains. They become depressed, unhappy. They feel small and insignificant.

But the strong, free soul expands and thrills before this testimony of God's artistry. On wings, it goes to meet a new beauty.

Altogether she is the most satisfying person I have met in the newer generations of Hollywood.

Her sophistication isn't superficial. It is a civilized understanding of the world, its ideals and its faults, its vice and its virtue. She can discuss such things in all their phases without prudery but also without vulgarity.

Del Rio is Mexican and fiery—when she wants to be. But it never runs away with her. The cross current of aristocratic Indian blood—she and Ramon Novarro are distant cousins and claim proudly a heritage from the great and wise Aztec chieftains—tempers the Mexican.

It gives her a cold, strong streak that is fascinating and creates the slightly haughty poise which makes her stand out.

Perhaps the misunderstanding—or rather the lack of understanding—comes from the contrast between her physical appearance and her actual character. I've never known anyone whose appearance was so deceptive.

DEL RIO looks orchidaceous. One imagines her in stately ballrooms, exquisite boudoirs, softly lighted drawing rooms. And in ballrooms and boudoirs she does very well. The way she wears her clothes, her many beautiful jewels, suggest that her being is centered in these feminine idols. You think of perfumes, bath salts, filmy négligées, French maids. True, she has all those things and loves them.

They are part of her charm, they are so feminine.

But they are only one side of Del Rio. And though the best known side, the most exploited, relatively unimportant to her and to any true understanding of her.

TOM MIX once said to me: "It takes a big man to live in big places. Little men can't stand the contrast. They are afraid."

In my opinion it is a rare woman who, with only one woman companion, seeks the lofty loneliness of the Sierras for weeks at a time.

Hiking those mountain trails is no easy thing for any woman. It takes wind and muscles in perfect condition. It takes heart and stamina.

Del Rio has that sort of hardness, mentally and physically.

Thus you have two sides—the orchid, and the woman who loves big and strong things of the outdoors.

But there are other sides.

Not so long ago Colleen Moore and Leatrice Joy and Dolores Del Rio and I occupied a table for four at Diana Fitzmaurice's shower for Bebe Daniels.

We got so uproarious that it was disgraceful. I never saw anyone laugh with such gusto as Dolores. There was the warm, emotional Latin, taking her merriment like a child.

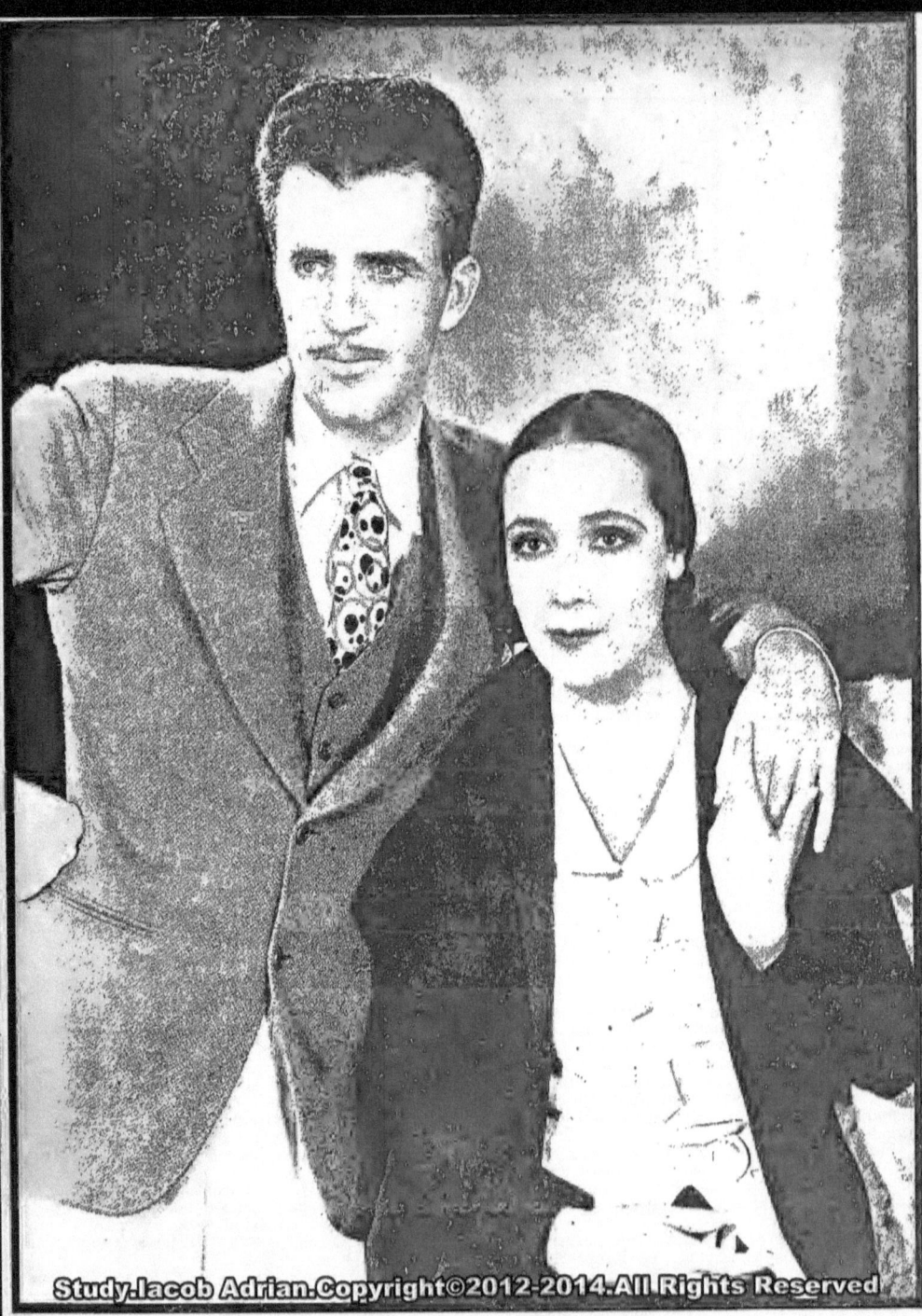

Presenting Mr. and Mrs. Cedric Gibbons. Mrs. Gibbons, of course, is known to you as Dolores Del Rio. Mr. Gibbons and Miss Del Rio were married in the famous Santa Barbara Mission in the midst of the annual Fiesta. Their wedding in the old Spanish town, glowing with the blooms of the flowering eucalyptus trees and purple acacias, had the flavor of old-time romance. They spent their honeymoon at Santa Barbara, watching the Fiesta, and in Monterey.

Dolores Gets Married

DARLING:

There just never has been anything so *romantic* as Dolores Del Rio's wedding to Cedric Gibbons.

After Bebe and Sally were married I thought you couldn't have a real wedding without a long veil and a lot of lovely bridesmaids. But I've changed my mind. Dolores' wedding was like something out of an old romance and it was just *perfect*.

I wish you could have been there, darling, because you do love romantic things so much, but since you had to stay in New York this year, I'll try to make you feel you did see it all.

THEY were married in the Santa Barbara Mission by Father Augustine, one of the Franciscan monks.

Santa Barbara is one of the most beautiful towns in the world. And Dolores and Cedric drove up there to be married. You know Cedric is rated as the finest art director in motion pictures, and is really an excellent artist himself. Besides, he is an Irish gentleman, educated in Dublin, and loves to do things in a dashing way. Just look how he swept Dolores off her feet. You know she said she'd never marry again. Then she met Cedric at a party at Marion Davies' house.

It was certainly love at first sight with Cedric, because I was sitting next to him at dinner that night and he really could hardly speak, for looking at Dolores, who was in a simple, black gown. I didn't mind because that nice Gene Markey was on my right and you know he talks all the time, so it was all right. Finally Cedric got up nerve enough to ask Dolores to dance and just a few weeks later they were engaged. He was the kind of a suitor girls dream about, so sweet and attentive and always doing lovely things for her. And, of course, he is *brilliant*. Besides being so distinguished-looking.

They drove up to Santa Barbara, through those wonderful orange groves. And Santa Barbara is just like an old Spanish town. All the buildings are early California and this time of year the flowering eucalyptus trees and the purple acacias are all in bloom. You never saw such masses of color and such beautiful flowers everywhere, just as though the town itself had been all decorated for a bridal party.

But added to that, it was the week of the Santa Barbara Fiesta, which is one of the glorious sights of California. For a week, everyone tries to bring back the days of early California, and the streets are full of pretty girls and young men dressed in Spanish costumes, and wonderful horses with silver saddles, and old coaches drawn by white horses with hammered silver harnesses. They have dances and parades and everything—and people come from all over the world to see it.

SO you can imagine how Dolores and Cedric felt, driving through those beautiful streets and Dolores looked as though she were the Spanish princess chosen to be queen of the Fiesta, as they did in the old days. On all sides there was music, guitars and Spanish tunes, and caballeros singing serenades under balconies covered with flowers.

Of course, the jewel of the whole town is the Santa Barbara Mission, which is on a low hill, just in back of the town and which was built by Father Junipero Serra in 1786. It has been restored and kept in wonderful condition so it looks just as it did then. Around it are lovely gardens and it is simply exquisite to look at.

Just a small party went up with Dolores, because she said when she decided to be married quietly in Santa Barbara and couldn't have a big wedding, she would just have her closest friends and not try to have guests. So there was Dolores and Cedric, and Mrs. Asunsolo, Dolores' mother, who was her only attendant, and Mr. and Mrs. Don Alvarado—Anne Alvarado is Dolores' best friend and almost like a sister—

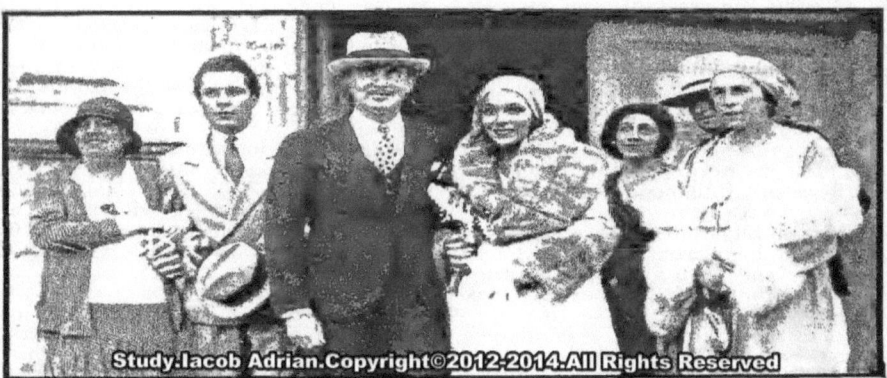

Dolores Del Rio and Cedric Gibbons in front of the historic old Mission in Santa Barbara, following their marriage by the Reverend Father Augustine. The wedding party, from left to right: Mrs. Sidney Toler, a friend of the bride's mother, Don Alvarado, Mr. and Mrs. Gibbons, Mrs. Don Alvarado, Benjamin Glazer, the best man, and Mrs. J. L. Asunsolo, mother of Dolores and matron of honor.

Dolores Gets Married

and Barney Glazer, who is Cedric's best friend, and Mrs. Toler, who is Dolores' mother's best friend.

THEY went to the darling El Mirasol Hotel first. You know that's where I was married. There, too, George Fitzmaurice and Diana Kane were wed. It has lots of pleasant memories. It's a divine spot, a lot of little Spanish bungalows in the midst of gardens and trees, and would make you feel romantic even if you weren't.

Well, they expected to be married at noon, but they couldn't be. Even that was romantic and like a play, because for a while it looked as though maybe they couldn't be married at all. You see, they are both Catholics. Dolores is very devout, being brought up in a convent and all. And at first the Father thought he couldn't marry them in the church because Dolores had been married before and divorced. But you see her first husband, Jaime Del Rio, died, so finally it was all right.

So, at five o'clock, they drove up to the Mission and people all along the streets threw flowers at them and showered blessings upon them in Spanish.

The Mission steps are all worn smooth with the feet that have passed. Many of the beautiful Spanish girls who were there in the early days must have gone up those steps to be married before that very altar. But I know there never was a lovelier bride than Dolores.

SHE wore a gown of the palest soft gray crêpe, with a long coat to match, trimmed with an enormous collar of gray squirrel. It was just off white, really, darling, and just the perfect thing for an informal wedding. On the collar she had pinned a spray of dark red roses and lilies-of-the-valley and you can imagine how becoming they were to her dark beauty. Her hat was the softest felt and exactly matched her dress and was very severe, relieved only by a small diamond pin.

Of course Cedric wore the conventional dark blue suit, but really, darling, he is handsome. He has black curly hair and Irish eyes of blue gray and a little mustache. They did look a stunning couple.

The rest of the party was simply dressed, because Dolores insisted that as it was a simple, informal wedding no one must be out of character. Anne Alvarado was in very dark blue, and Mrs. Asunsolo wore a pale blue suit.

The lovely old chapel was dim with candlelight and the big organ played softly as they walked down the aisle.

There were only a few people in the church, kneeling at their prayers. At the altar, Father Augustine waited. You know the monks at the Santa Barbara Mission still wear the old Franciscan habit, dark brown flowing robes, with a cord tied around the waist. You've seen pictures of the blessed Father Junipero Serra, who founded all the California Missions, and they look now just as he did then.

So they were married by the priest with the beautiful Catholic ceremony. Dolores' accent sounded so sweet in that setting and Cedric was wonderful, though he was just as white as a sheet, but I'm sure it wasn't fear but some much more beautiful emotion, because he is simply mad about Dolores, and who can blame him? He was certainly a lucky man to get her.

As they came back down the aisle a little old Mexican woman in a mantilla who was saying her rosary got up and gave them a blessing in Spanish.

THEY went back to the El Mirasol, where a wedding supper had been prepared in their bungalow, which was simply one mass of gorgeous flowers. And then the rest of the party came back to Los Angeles and Mr. and Mrs. Cedric Gibbons stayed to see the Fiesta and join in it as part of their honeymoon. And later they went up to Monterey and spent a week. That's another beautiful old Spanish town, so they kept right in the spirit of it all.

Now they're home and are living in Cedric's new home at Santa Monica. Wasn't it amazing that he started to build it before he even met Dolores and it was done just the day they were married and they were able to return to it, all new and lovely, and start their married life together there. Dolores is going to keep house in Hollywood and they'll use that for a town house in the winter.

Honestly, I don't know what we shall do if everyone keeps having these lovely weddings. It will ruin Hollywood's reputation for being a wild town full of nothing but scandals, won't it? Of course, we all know a good deal of that is exaggerated.

I'm sure Dolores and Cedric are going to be happy. He understands her and will join in the fun she wants, and he's got a grand sense of humor, which is one of the things Dolores adores.

I hope if we have another wedding soon you can come out for it. Because weddings really are *swell*, as my adorable Ruth Chatterton would say,

All my love, angel, from your devoted daughter.

The SUPPRESSED Desires of the STARS

Even as You and I, the Hollywood Favorites Long to do Something Else

BY HARRY D. WILSON

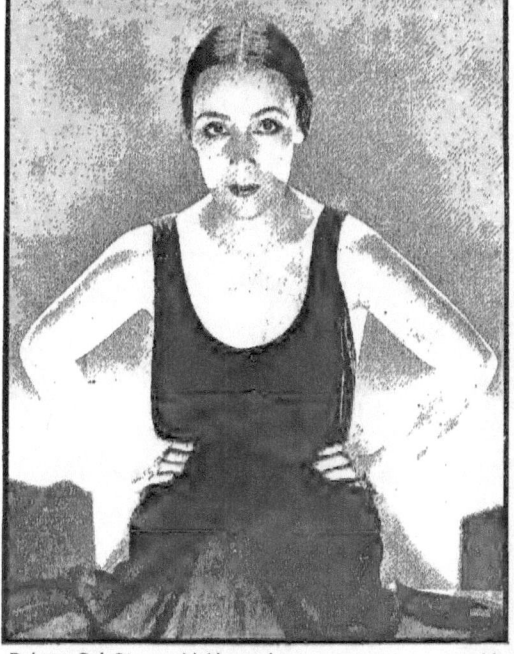

Dolores Del Rio would like to be a great actress, capable of swaying vast audiences. Most of all she would like to possess Bernhardt's golden voice or Duse's eloquent hands.

SUPPRESSED desires! What lure—what thrills; flights in imagery; what heights and depths these words convey. A king wishes he were a plow boy. A plow boy dreams of ruling a kingdom. And so it goes.

In Hollywood, where a twist of fate turns a struggling extra overnight to the dazzling honors of stardom—where stars of the moment suddenly find themselves pushed into the realms of the forgotten, desires that are thought, not even breathed, possess the bosoms of the great, near-great and the lowliest.

Pola Negri, glowing with anticipation of the future, sat and talked of suppressed desires that brought her triumphantly through years of torture to the threshold of a new career.

"One outstanding triumph—an artistic achievement so great it will send my name ringing down the ages—that is my great desire," said Pola. "To give richly of the talent God gave me, as Rockefeller might give his millions. When I have accomplished this, my great happiness would be to revert to a normal life—a life in which the right kind of marriage could have its place—one which would give the most understanding companionship. You know, most marriages are founded on sex attraction. How wrong that is. What a mistake. Sex has nothing to do with love. That I have learned. Nothing! Love is

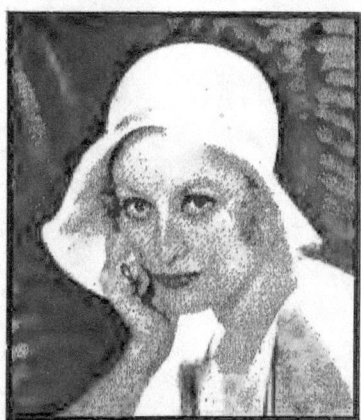

Joan Crawford would like to give up acting to be a sculptress. To produce great things in clay, that, at present, is her hidden ambition.

a thing apart—a lasting, sharing, understanding quality that can be defined a thousand ways, but remains the same. Sex is merely incidental—a lure of nature for the unsuspecting. Sometimes it proves love's greatest enemy.

"To gain real love I may have to find a man older than I on whom to lean—to soothe me from the experiences with which ambition has strewn my troubled path. It's ambition that drives me to the realization of these desires. Men have almost ruined my career but the urge for fame saved me. To regain strength from my marital misfortune, I sought simplicity of living on my farm in France. There I dwelt close to the earth. From it came renewed desires."

These words flowed in an intense stream from the lips of a woman who can truly be termed "of the universe." Born in Poland, her struggles to fulfill her chosen career forced her to become immersed in the rhythm of the world. A woman of strange contradictions — one moment exotic—another simple—but always generous.

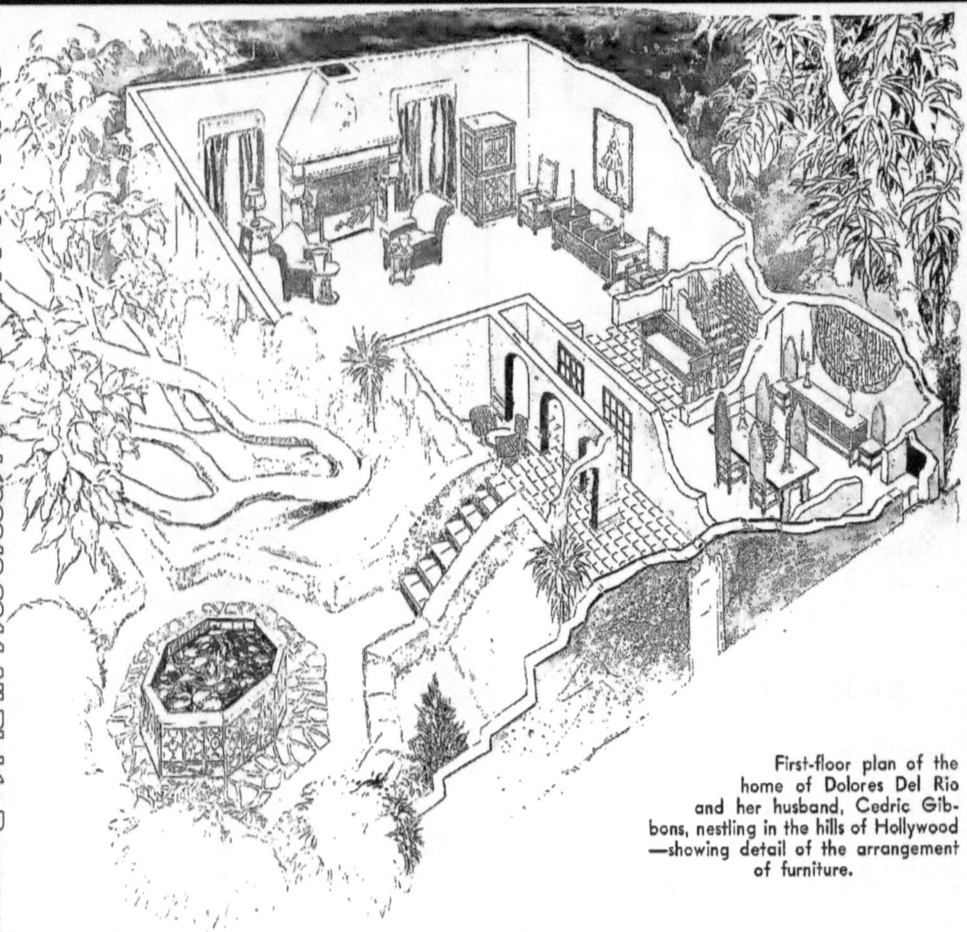

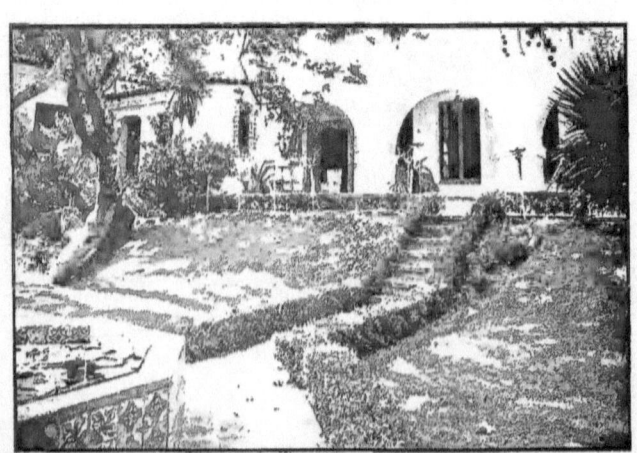

First-floor plan of the home of Dolores Del Rio and her husband, Cedric Gibbons, nestling in the hills of Hollywood —showing detail of the arrangement of furniture.

Dolores Del Rio At Home

Another Feature in this illuminating series depicting the Hollywood houses of the stars and how they are furnished

THE Hollywood Hills home of Dolores Del Rio in the ultra-fashionable Outpost Estates was designed from her own plans five years ago, and furnished with great care, over a period of at least two years, by Miss Del Rio herself.

The south front of Dolores Del Rio's beautiful Hollywood home.

Few film-star homes have so much of the personal selection and taste of the star represented, and so little of the pro-

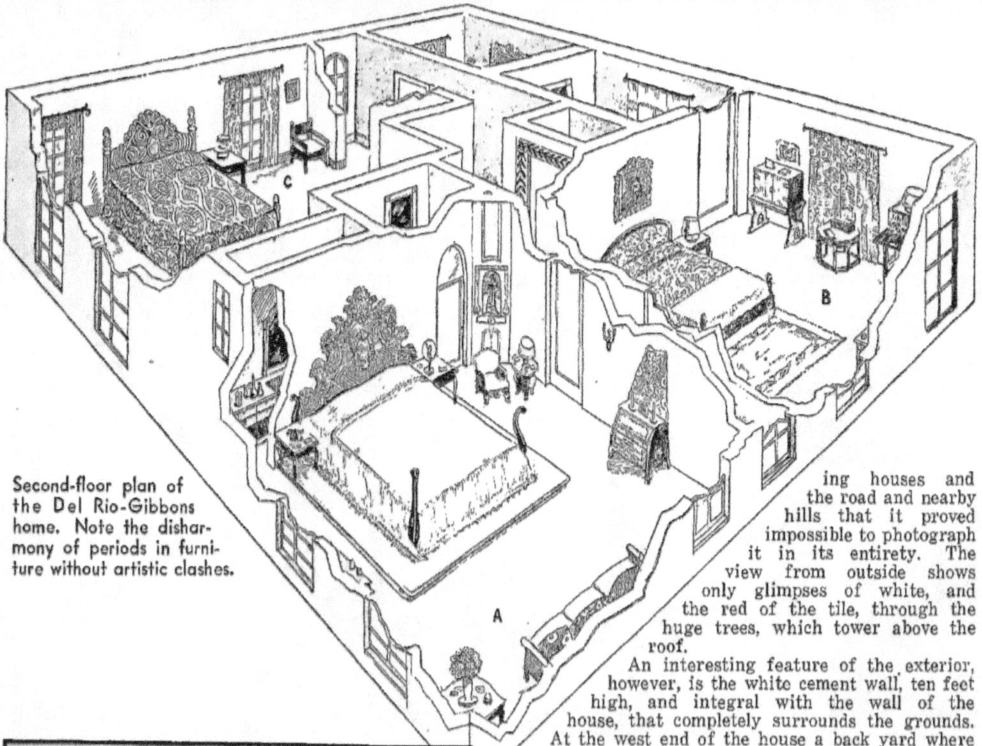

Second-floor plan of the Del Rio-Gibbons home. Note the disharmony of periods in furniture without artistic clashes.

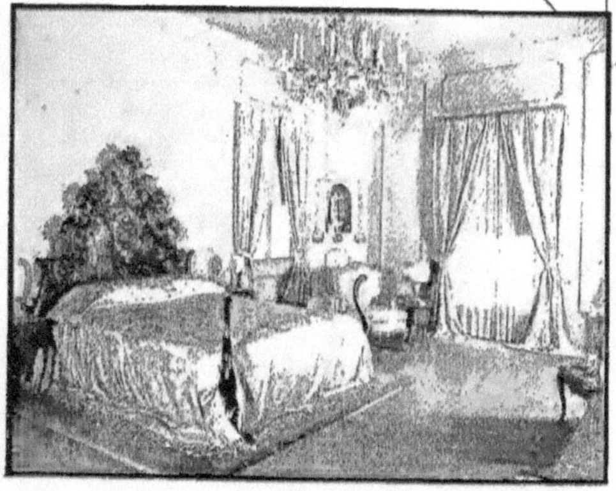

ing houses and the road and nearby hills that it proved impossible to photograph it in its entirety. The view from outside shows only glimpses of white, and the red of the tile, through the huge trees, which tower above the roof.

An interesting feature of the exterior, however, is the white cement wall, ten feet high, and integral with the wall of the house, that completely surrounds the grounds.

At the west end of the house a back yard where one may take sun baths; this spot is also walled off from the main yard, which contains the trees, patio, fountain and walks, best depicted by the accompanying photographs.

A piazza with Moorish arches and seats of pink Moorish tile, floored with red cement blocks, runs the length of the house on its frontage south. The street entrance is through a Mission-style door opening from the east street frontage to the piazza directly.

THE big Moorish door opening to the reception room of the house discloses the latter as equally Moorish, from its iron-work stairway, red-tile-block floor and elaborate red tiling on the wall to its extension from

Gibbons' Moorish and Spanish style bedroom. The rug is dark brown, the walls tan, the furniture mahogany, as is the woodwork finish. The bedspread is dark red, with figures of dull gold.

Light and air flood Dolores Del Rio's boudoir, which is decorated in harmonizing tans and gold.

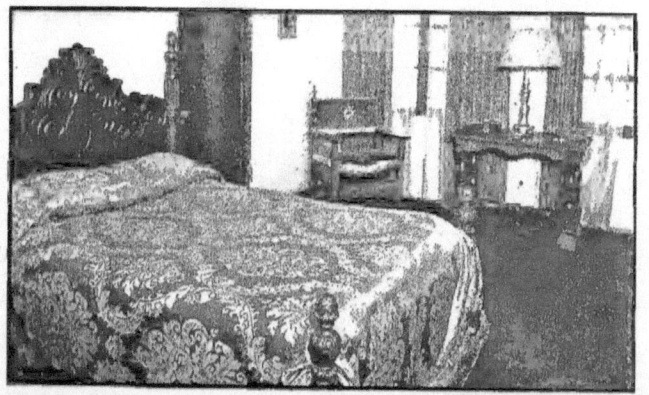

fessional interior decorator and architect. Almost the same thing might be said of the grounds. Miss Del Rio selected a general location she liked north of Hollywood, at the foot of the hills. She found a corner lot large enough for her purpose. It was wooded with some artistically sprawling sycamore trees. With this basis she laid plans for her present white-stucco, Spanish-style, red-tile-roofed house.

The house itself is two-story. Including servants' quarters, it contains fifteen rooms. Yet it is so completely hidden from surround-

the ground floor to the second-story roof, with a beamed ceiling.

Two steps below the reception room level, and at the left as you enter the house—that is, toward the west frontage—is the big living-room, which extends its length from north to south, with sunny windows on the south and west sides. This room is uniformly Moorish in furnishing except for plaques on the walls—a feature of the entire place, the plaques being of Spanish kings—and some modern chairs and over-stuffed furniture for greater comfort.

On the west wall is a huge fireplace. The Moorish effect is carried out in tapestry, in the beamed ceiling, the severe drapes and shades, the massive table, and the prevalence of wrought-iron work, including a massive chandelier.

At the opposite end of the reception room or hall, which runs east and west, is the dining room, furnished in the Spanish style which shows such a marked combination of Moorish and Italian influence. The massive table is Moorish, the chairs Spanish-Italian,

Mr. Gibbons' room is severely Moorish, while the guest room is a pleasing mixture of periods, into which fit with color harmony and pleasing effect such things as a huge llama robe on the bed, and a black and tan white fur rug.

In every way, Miss Del Rio's home reveals what may be done by discarding conventions of period and style, and letting taste dictate the arrangement of a room. Individuality and a distinctive type of beauty is the result.

IT is interesting to know that Miss Del Rio scorned the usual custom of Hollywood stars in resorting to the "interior decorator." Hollywood customarily turns to the "interior decorator" when it accomplishes the "new house."

There is the classic story of the little lady of sudden fame whose Cinderella-like jump to prosperity from long, lean years in the extra-girl class brewed within her the longing for "a little place in the hills" which should compare in magnificence and costliness with the

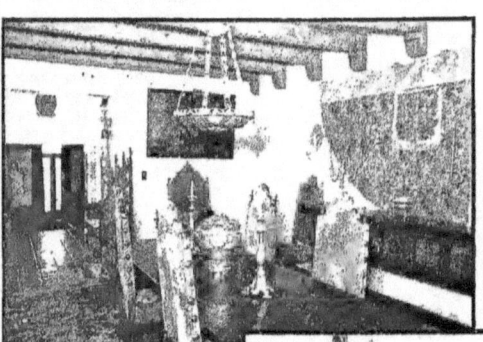

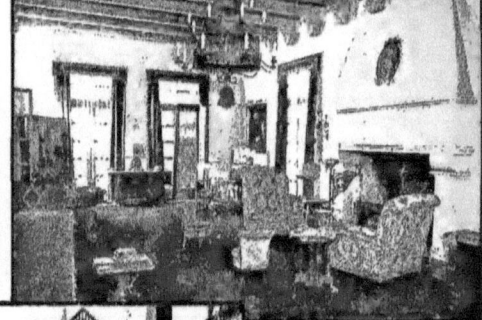

The dining-room is Italian with Moorish influence, seen in the beam ceilings and the inlay on the sideboard. The colorings are tan, red and gold.

The living-room. Looking south toward the French windows that open to the garden. Note the wrought-iron, Moorish light and fireplace fixtures.

the drapes Italian. The color scheme is one of rich reds and browns.

OPENING through a little telephone-room alcove or miniature hall from the reception hall, just to the left of the outer door and between it and the living room, is a den of Georgian and Old English influence,

The two-story reception hall—or entrance hall—of Dolores Del Rio's Hollywood home. It is strictly Moorish in style, with its red cement block floors and its red and white tiles, except for the Spanish plaques on the walls.

homes of the stars who had lorded it over her for so long.

With no discredit to her, she had come to Hollywood from the farthest steppes of Chicago. Her previous income taxes had been paid, if any, from her earnings as a saleswoman at Marshal Fields'. She had sold furniture and had dreams of

surprising in this house—cabinet-work, paneled walls, shelves supporting bits of Dresden, comfortable chairs and tables for reading, and, of course, shelves of books.

Now go up the stairs to the second-story hallway, which runs the length of the house from east to west. Baths and closets open to the north, also a maid's room. At the east end is the big, beautifully furnished bedroom of the star herself, and at the other end, the guest bedroom. Adjoining Miss Del Rio's room, but south of the hallway, is that of her husband, Cedric Gibbons.

Miss Del Rio's room is so intimately her own that she totally disregarded periods and all but her own taste in combining its Venetian bed, massive and elaborately carved, with a French chandelier, an Oriental commode, French chairs, some modern chairs—even a touch of the Italian and Spanish. She blended the styles so artfully that the room is a thing of beauty.

her own. One of these dreams was of chairs that could be taken apart and folded up.

Like Miss Del Rio, she found a charming plot of ground on a hillside. She found the architect who would design her house. With a hundred-thousand-dollar-a-year contract, she worried not a whit about the cost of things. She designed her own house, and it is one of the most beautifully laid out houses in Hollywood. The girl should have been an architect!

But she could not design folding chairs in period style. She engaged an "interior decorator." Her only instruction was that her home should be "Old English," which meant Heppelwhite and Adams and Sheraton, and that the drawing-room chairs should be put together so they could be taken down.

The result proves that Miss Del Rio could be an "interior decorator" herself if she should tire being the exotic Dolores of the screen.

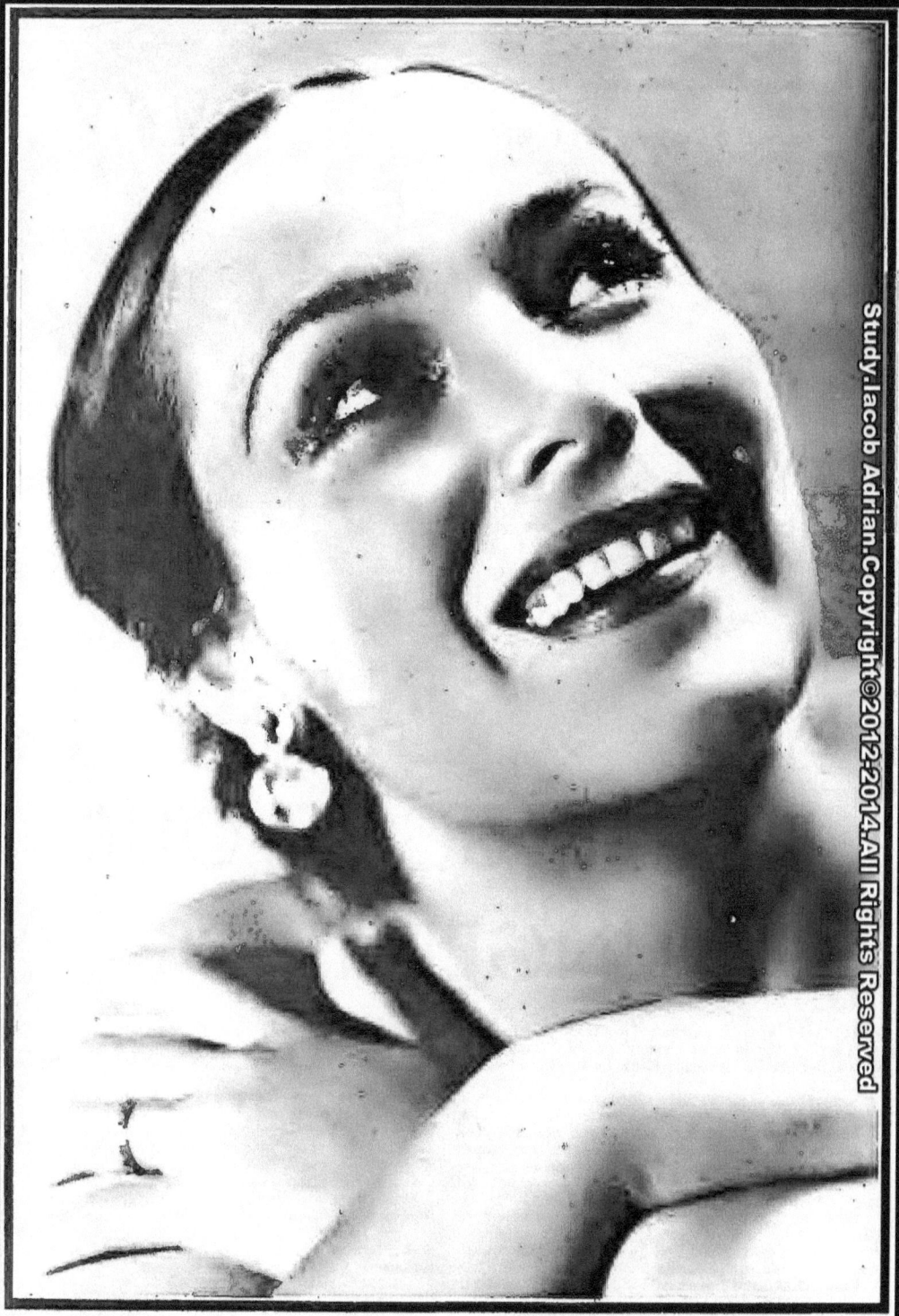

DOLORES DEL RIO

A woman's good breeding is reflected in the care she gives her hands,

says DOLORES DEL RIO

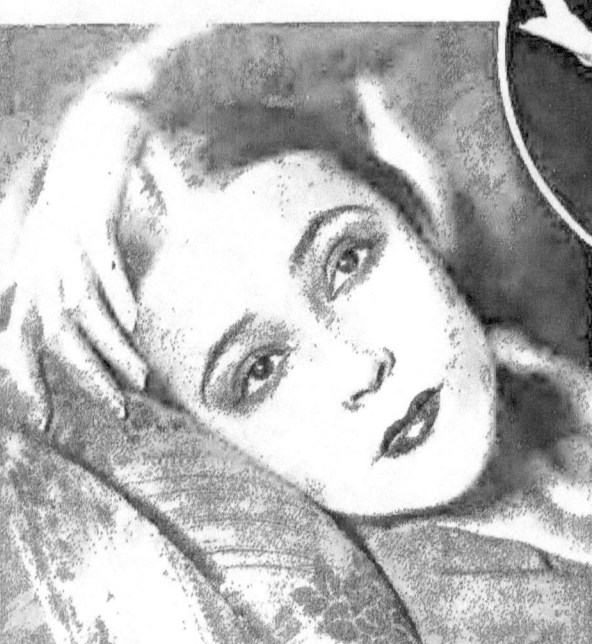

Dolores' hands in closeup,
beautifully cared for and expressive of her personality
and changing moods.

Languor is the pose here,
and is as well expressed by
Dolores' drooping fingers as
by her calm face (for the
moment) and dreamy eyes.

BEAUTIFUL to YOUR FINGER-TIPS

"WITH the possible exception of her eyes, no feature of woman's loveliness has inspired such lyric enthusiasm as shapely, graceful hands," declares Dolores Del Rio, sparkling Latin star of RKO-Radio pictures.

"Hands express character in so many ways. And they may express the type of character we wish them to have to a certain extent. Certainly a woman's good breeding is reflected in the care she gives her hands. Hands that naturally assume graceful poses are enhanced by perfect grooming, and awkward hands are less noticeable when they are well cared for."

Miss Del Rio's slim hands with their long-tipped nails are an essential part of her allure. She knows how to use them to their best advantage. They are always an integral part of the picture she presents.

The first essential, of course, she believes is absolute cleanliness. Daintiness should be basic here as in every other characteristic of a well-groomed woman.

"Never have a disagreeable smudge mar the perfection of your hands. If ink stains the fingers while writing, scrub them immediately and if necessary follow with a light bleach to remove the spot. Lemon juice or one of the prepared bleaches with handy little applicators will do the trick for you. Dust gathers on anyone's hands in the course of any daily routine, but that is no excuse for letting it remain."

Dolores recommends rubbing the hands with a good softening lotion morning and night—one that tends to tighten the skin somewhat, giving a smooth, velvety surface. This is especially good for hands susceptible to chapping, and should be applied just before going outdoors and after washing the hands at any time.

Hands that are rough and lumpy will be immensely improved by massage with a good nourishing or tissue cream. Improved in appearance and in grace as well. A tired, nervous hand is never as graceful or as expressive.

"THERE is no excuse for unpleasant and unsightly hangnails. Prevent them by massaging the cuticle about the nails with a cotten-wrapped orange-wood stick dipped in oil. Olive oil is effective, as are several of the cuticle oils and creams on the

Beautiful to Your Finger-Tips

market. A nightly application of oil rubbed gently around the cuticle of each nail before retiring will keep them healthy and firm and in perfect condition.

"Don't have your nails manicured carelessly. Just because pointed nails look well on the hands of your neighbor is no reason why they will become your own fingers which are shaped totally differently. Study the size and type of your hands before deciding to wear your nails oval or pointed, short or fairly long.

"Colored nail polish is another item that should be approached with discretion. Bright vermilion nails may be suitable with certain hands and with certain personalities, but they are not in good taste for every one."

THE girl who does her own manicure should keep in touch with expert practice by going to a manicurist occasionally and carefully watching the process. And the woman who does her own housework can keep her hands from showing it if, in addition to spending five minutes morning and night on them, she wears rubber gloves while working at household tasks. These gloves will prove to her one of the best investments she ever made.

"It's not an elaborate process," says Dolores, "this keeping the hands in the pink of condition. The morning and evening minutes dedicated to them, plus frequent washings in between time followed by application of lotion, and a weekly manicure, will work wonders for any pair of hands. Then it's up to the woman to show off these lovely hands she has achieved to their best advantage."

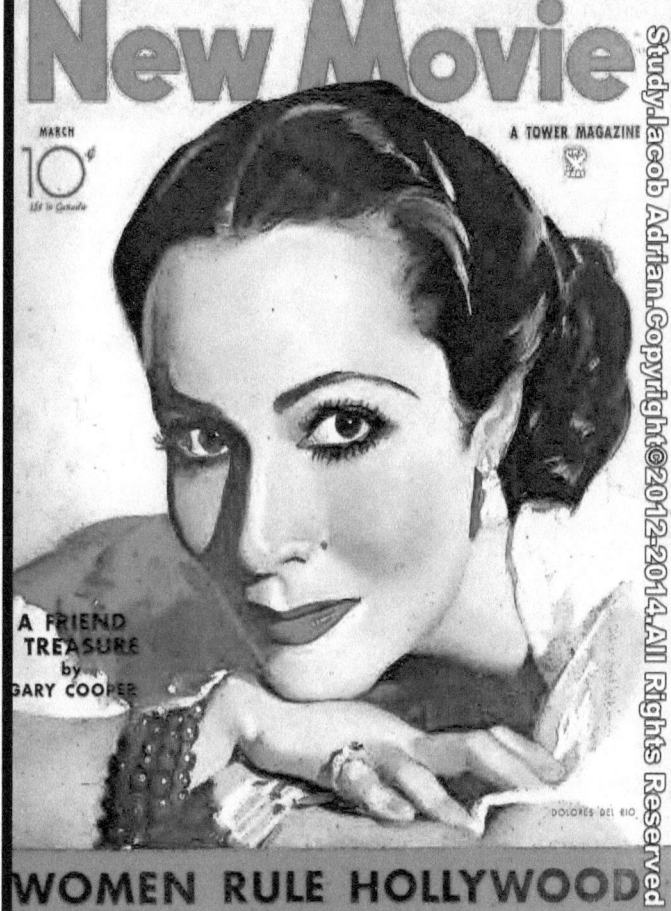

NEW Movie

A TOWER MAGAZINE

MARCH

10¢

15¢ in Canada

A FRIEND TREASURE by GARY COOPER

DOLORES DEL RIO

WOMEN RULE HOLLYWOOD

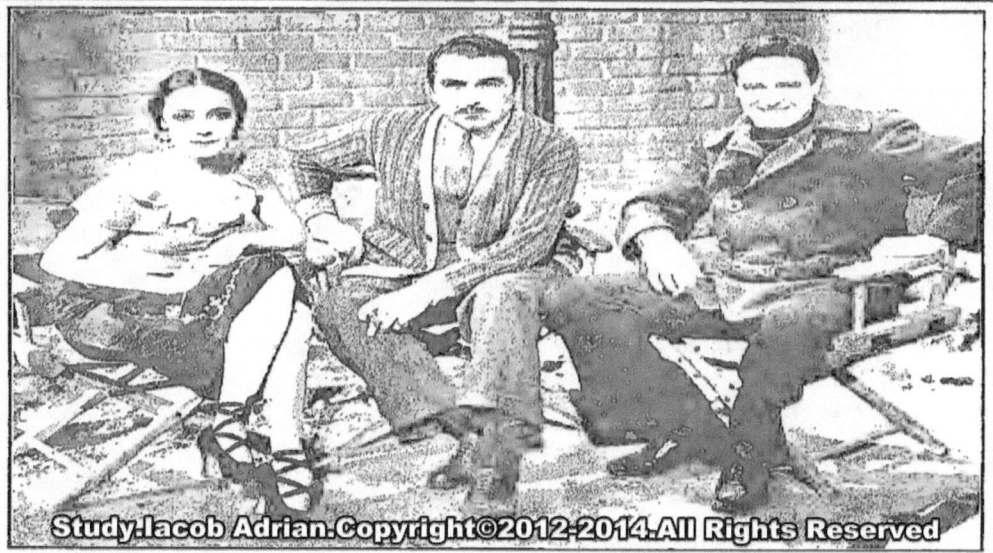

Between scenes of "The Bad One," in which Dolores Del Rio plays a daring role far afield from her recent mild screen heroines. In the picture are Miss Del Rio, Director George Fitzmaurice, who made "The Bad One," and Edmund Lowe, who appears opposite the Mexican actress.

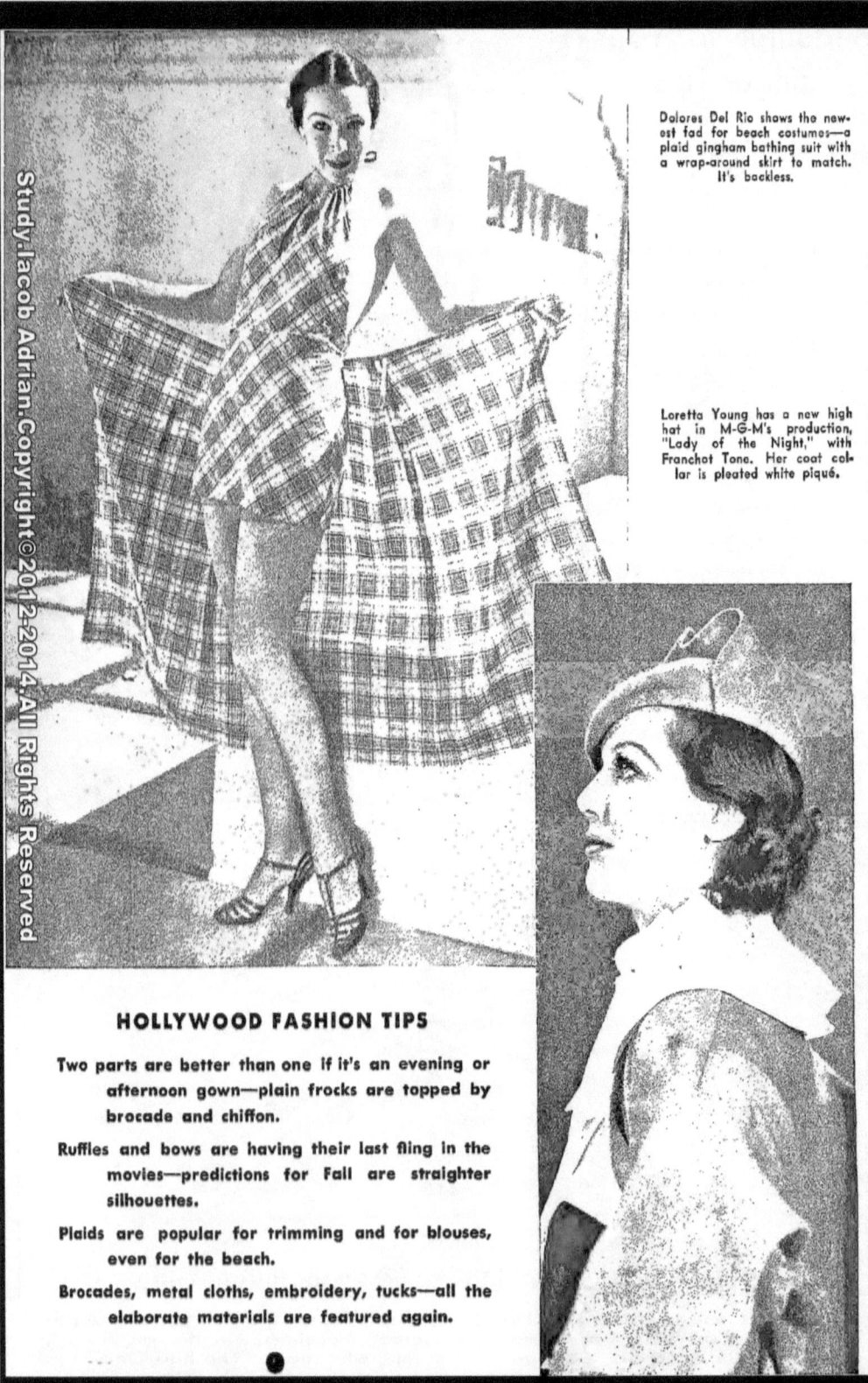

Dolores Del Rio shows the newest fad for beach costumes—a plaid gingham bathing suit with a wrap-around skirt to match. It's backless.

Loretta Young has a new high hat in M-G-M's production, "Lady of the Night," with Franchot Tone. Her coat collar is pleated white piqué.

HOLLYWOOD FASHION TIPS

Two parts are better than one if it's an evening or afternoon gown—plain frocks are topped by brocade and chiffon.

Ruffles and bows are having their last fling in the movies—predictions for Fall are straighter silhouettes.

Plaids are popular for trimming and for blouses, even for the beach.

Brocades, metal cloths, embroidery, tucks—all the elaborate materials are featured again.

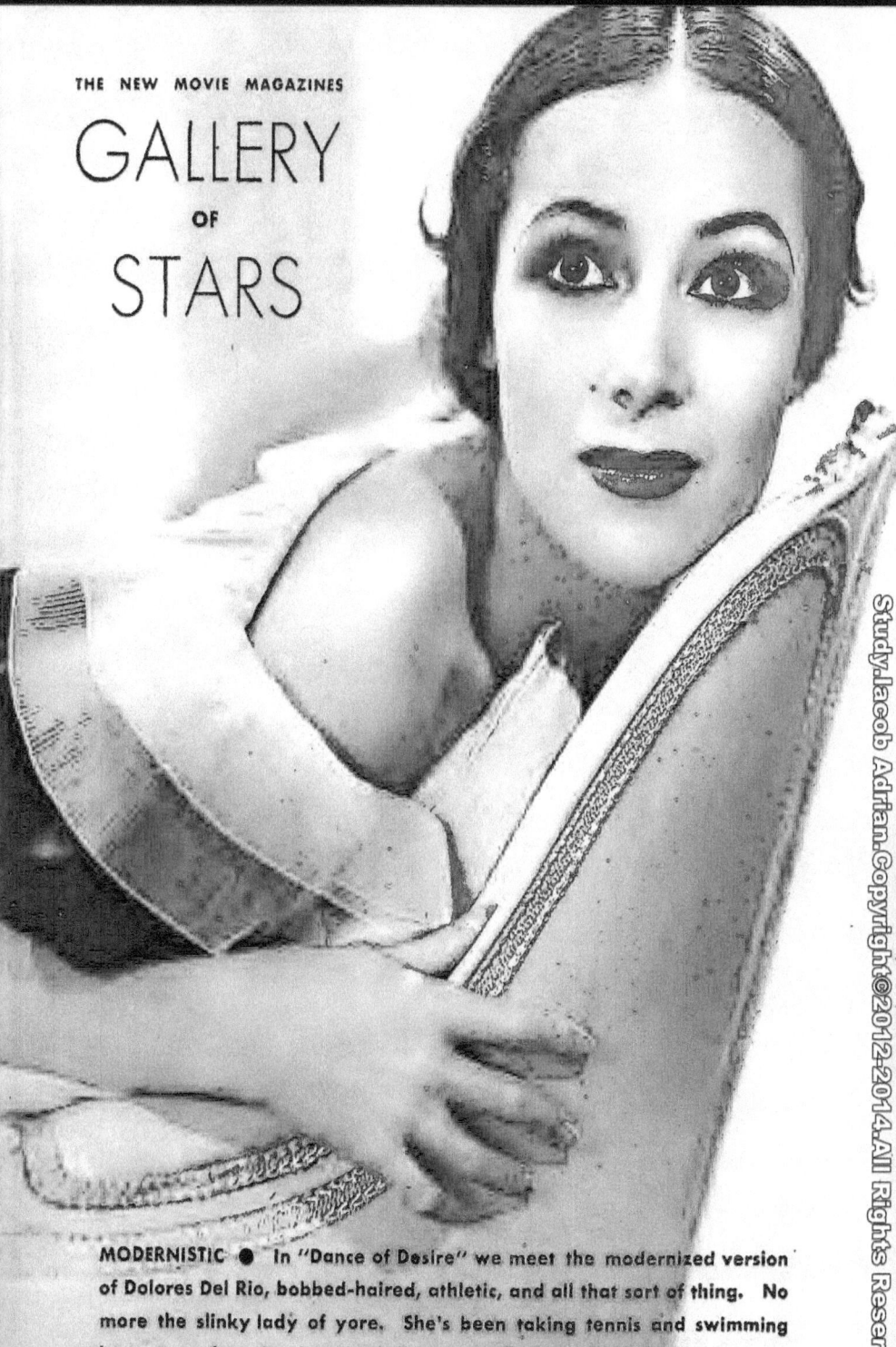

THE NEW MOVIE MAGAZINES

GALLERY

OF

STARS

MODERNISTIC ● In "Dance of Desire" we meet the modernized version of Dolores Del Rio, bobbed-haired, athletic, and all that sort of thing. No more the slinky lady of yore. She's been taking tennis and swimming lessons, modern dancing and being generally brought up to date . . .

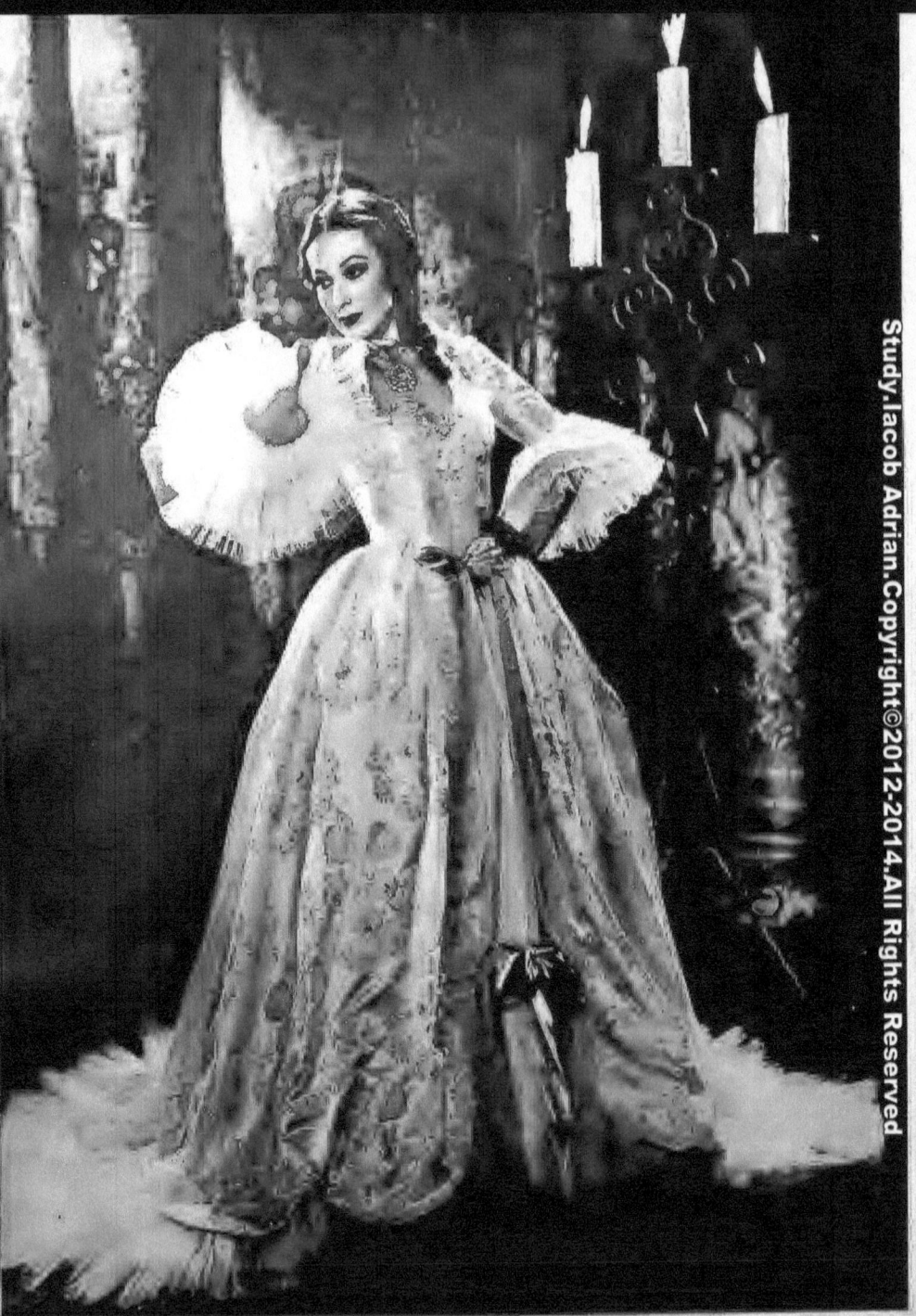

DOLORES DEL RIO—Have you considered Dolores a type, doomed forever to play Spanish charmers with the aid of fan and mantilla? Wrong again—and the producers knew it. Next she will bow to you as Rima, the Bird Girl, in RKO's "Green Mansions" and will glide thence into the tempestuous role of DuBarry, in Warners' production of the same name.

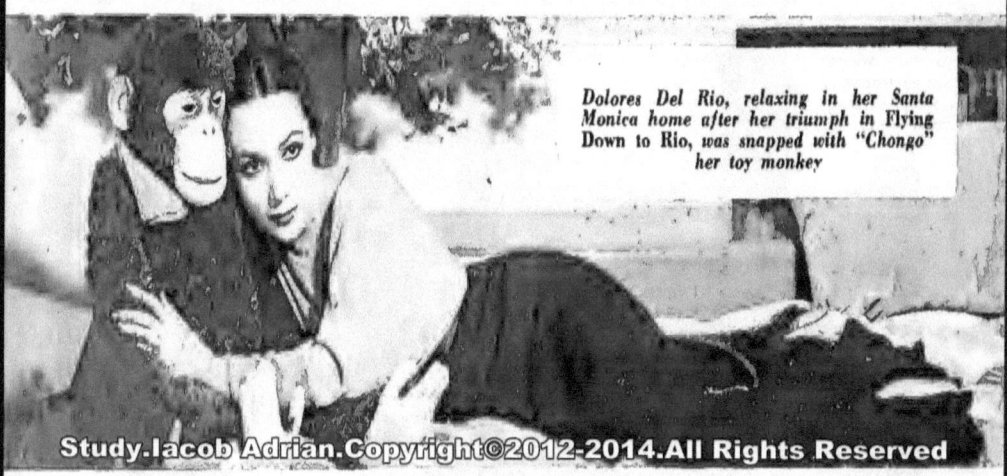

Dolores Del Rio, relaxing in her Santa Monica home after her triumph in Flying Down to Rio, was snapped with "Chongo" her toy monkey

■ Before leaving for the army, Joe Rivkin, a Hollywood agent, presented his best girl, Katharine Booth, with a bracelet engraved: "To Katharine, Remember Pearl Harbor—and Joe."

■ Diana Barrymore's role in Universal's *Love and Kisses—Caroline* will be the most unglamorous feminine role of the year. She'll portray a girl of 14 with braids, horn-rimmed glasses and braces on her teeth. It's the role Deanna Durbin turned down to escape the juvenile tag.

■ Gene Raymond's face is still red after flopping at a legerdemain trick at a dinner party before reporting to the army. Gene borrowed a large silk handkerchief from one of the guests and started the hocus pocus with a burning cigarette. He doesn't know what went wrong but instead of vanishing, the cigarette burned a big hole in the expensive handkerchief. "There was only one trick I wanted to know right then," says Gene, "and that was for me to disappear."

■ On a recent night clubbing expedition, Nancy Kelly wore a hunk of costume jewelry fashioned like a traffic signal, with small, colored stop and go lights operated by hidden batteries and controlled by a switch. Worked fine in keeping the playboys in check--until the red bulb burned out.

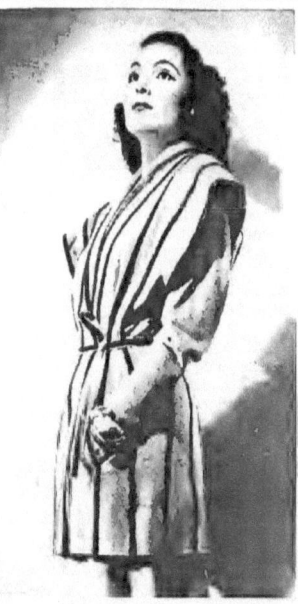

Dolores Del Rio returns to the screen after a long absence to star in Orson Welles' *Journey Into Fear*. Rumor has it that the dark, exotic actress, one of Hollywood's most beautiful women, will soon become Mrs. Orson Welles

■ Hollywood scenarists have written many stories of bravery but here is a real life story that tops them all. A year ago Vera Steadman, the famous silent day star, was struck by an automobile. Her back and both her legs were broken. Before operating, doctors said she had only a slight chance to live. And if she survived the operation, they said she'd probably be a cripple for life. The operation saved her life but Vera Steadman could not leave her hospital bed for six months. Four months ago she was released from the hospital in a wheel chair—a brace on her hip and braces on both legs. Doctors said she'd never walk again. But Vera Steadman didn't believe them. The other day, at a Los Angeles school for paralytics, I watched Vera Steadman walk again. It was a painful process but the pain will lessen each day. Vera Steadman will not be a cripple—thanks to bravery and determination far surpassing any movie plot.

■ Five years old, precocious Carolyn Lee asked her mother if she couldn't cut her hair for her role in *Mrs. Wiggs of the Cabbage Patch*. "Why?" asked mama. "It's too long," said Carolyn. "I'm afraid people might mistake me for Veronica Lake." Or so the story goes.

■ Dorothy Lamour's press agent has just figured out the sarong star is the champion "all-wet kissing heroine" in Hollywood.

· Dancing to Fame ·

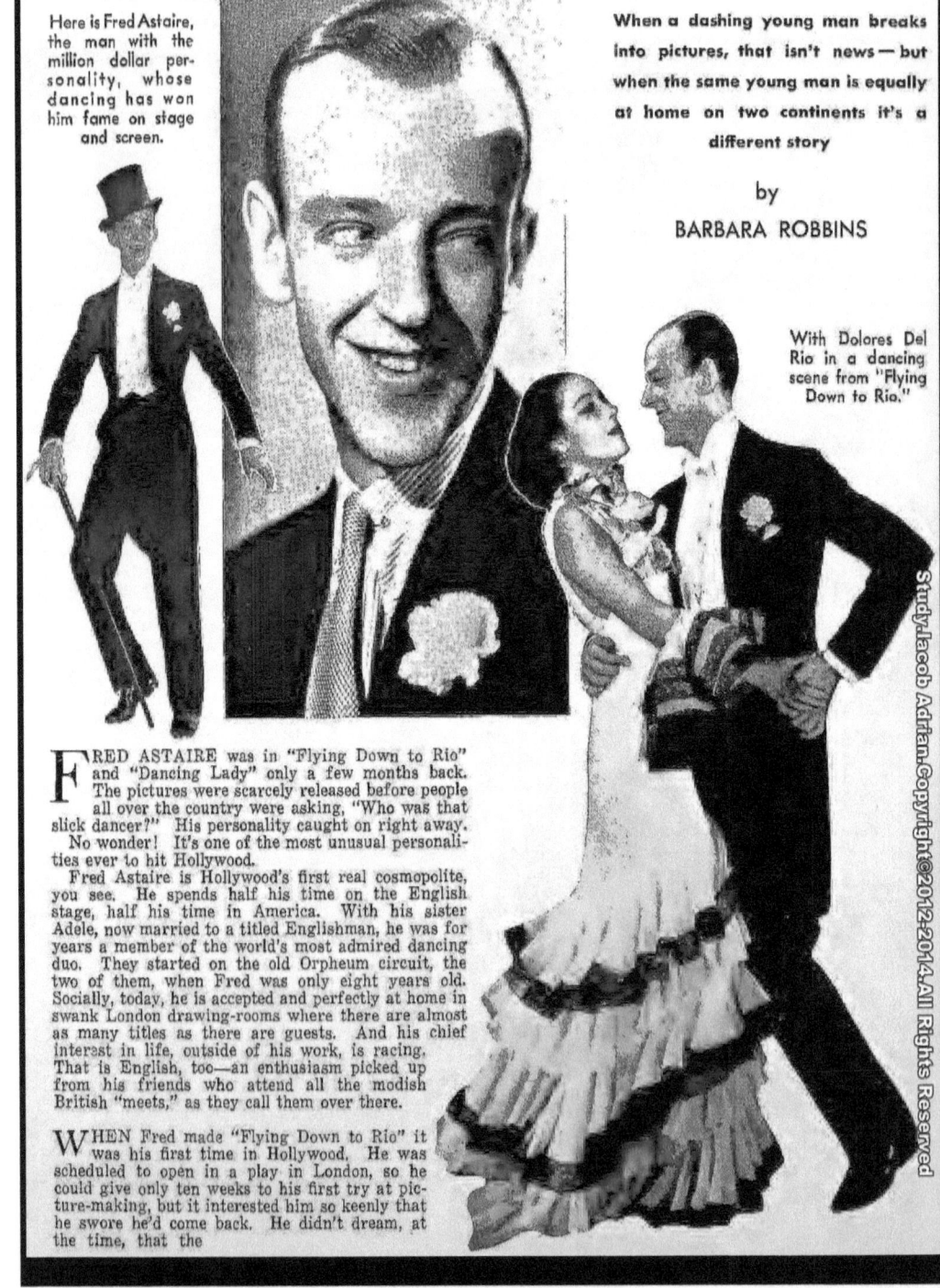

Here is Fred Astaire, the man with the million dollar personality, whose dancing has won him fame on stage and screen.

When a dashing young man breaks into pictures, that isn't news — but when the same young man is equally at home on two continents it's a different story

by

BARBARA ROBBINS

With Dolores Del Rio in a dancing scene from "Flying Down to Rio."

FRED ASTAIRE was in "Flying Down to Rio" and "Dancing Lady" only a few months back. The pictures were scarcely released before people all over the country were asking, "Who was that slick dancer?" His personality caught on right away. No wonder! It's one of the most unusual personalities ever to hit Hollywood.

Fred Astaire is Hollywood's first real cosmopolite, you see. He spends half his time on the English stage, half his time in America. With his sister Adele, now married to a titled Englishman, he was for years a member of the world's most admired dancing duo. They started on the old Orpheum circuit, the two of them, when Fred was only eight years old. Socially, today, he is accepted and perfectly at home in swank London drawing-rooms where there are almost as many titles as there are guests. And his chief interest in life, outside of his work, is racing. That is English, too—an enthusiasm picked up from his friends who attend all the modish British "meets," as they call them over there.

WHEN Fred made "Flying Down to Rio" it was his first time in Hollywood. He was scheduled to open in a play in London, so he could give only ten weeks to his first try at picture-making, but it interested him so keenly that he swore he'd come back. He didn't dream, at the time, that the

Dancing to Fame

But the following year, when they gave the charity bazaar in London again, Fred set up for himself a little booth in which he sold strawberries and cream.

THERE'S another story that he likes to tell. "The only way to get a good seat upstairs in a London theater is to come hours beforehand and wait in line on the sidewalk," he says. "They call it a queue. While you're standing there waiting men that they call queue entertainers stand in the street and sing songs and do juggling acts, hoping you'll toss them pennies. I'll never forget the time I heard a man sing a song called "Love and the Villain." He sang it with gestures that were gestures, and at the climax he pulled out a big revolver and waved it. It was just part of his act—but the whole queue ran down the street yelling murder, scared to death. When the theater opened there was nobody there to go in."

ALL his life Fred has been a rabid movie fan. That may have been what interested him in Hollywood in the first place. He likes George Raft. (He used to know him in the days when George was a hot Texas Tommy dancer in New York.) He has never missed a Cagney picture since the day he sat through Jimmy's "Public Enemy" three times. Gable he likes "just because he's Gable." And Bob Montgomery he admires for his charm and ease on the screen. . . . Of his favorites among the women stars, being a smart lad, he says nothing. "No Hair Pulling," is his motto.

But he never dreamed he'd be in the movies one day himself. And, after his experiences the first few days in the studios, he didn't want to be! You probably know what 'rushes' are. Every evening, after the day's work on the set, the laboratory rushes through a print of the day's shooting, so that the director and the doctors can study them in the projection room and decide what they're going to have to make all over again tomorrow. Fred didn't know that the rushes included all the bad takes of the day along with the good. He sat in the merciful darkness of the little projection room, his cheeks growing hotter and hotter, as he wincingly watched take after take unreel before him.

"I looked worse in every one of them," he groaned, remembering it. "Was I sick!"

ANOTHER thing horrified him when he saw the rushes on "Dancing Lady." While the motors are bringing the cameras up to speed, the actors often stand on the set making last-minute adjustments of neckties, stockings—if they're girls—and facial expressions. Fred didn't know about this either, yet. That is, he didn't realize that the cameras were picking all of it up, while they were getting up to speed. He didn't know that this part of the film would be cut off and thrown into the waste-basket in the cutting room. The result was, his first glimpse of himself in "Dancing Lady" was a vision of a gangling young man with his thumb down inside his collar and his face screwed up as though he were choking to death, trying to scratch his back with his free hand.

It took Joan Crawford to convince him that he wouldn't look that way on the screen. Joan and Franchot Tone, who are both his very good friends, were looking over the different rushes with him.

THINGS like that make Fred so miserable because he is one of the shyest human beings alive. Marriage to a stunning girl, the former Phyllis Potter, a society girl—money, friends for whom a social climber would give her diamond-encircled right arm, success in two countries, none of that helps. He is still shy. So shy that he is afraid to go to parties where he will meet strangers. So shy that his friends, who know about it, never ask him to perform for them in their homes. Even when he gives a performance for charity it has to be in a regular theater, to put the footlights between him and the audience as a barrier to keep them apart. It is this same shyness, showing on the screen no matter how much he tries to hide it, that makes us realize his inherent modesty and good-heartedness. That is one reason, no doubt, why we have taken to him so. The other is that it is so easy to see how much he enjoys dancing; loves it devotedly, and would go right on being a dancing comedian if he had ten million dollars. He doesn't work for money, he works for fun, and we all like that.

"I get a lot of fun out of working in pictures," he says grinning. "But I think of myself as an unknown quantity. I'm not sure myself, yet, I'm not at all sure that I'll be any good on the screen. I have to show myself that I am, first.

"I LOVE the stage, too, and I want to go on with my work there. But pictures are fascinating, there's no doubt about that. They have so much variety! I don't mind the waiting around for hours between shots. Lots of people do, but the waits give me time to think about the next scene. Just think, in a play, we rehearse for five weeks, try the thing out for a couple of weeks out of town, and even then we're not sure what it's going to be. That's real waiting! And then, when the play gets going for a long run, we do the same thing over and over, night after night, for months. In pictures you give your very best—once—and your best is what people see on the screen."

ENTHUSIASTIC, excitable, crammed with comedy, Fred Astaire is that rarest of the rare, a genuinely new personality for us. His comedy is never forced. It springs from the way he looks at life, himself. It's the same sense of humor that made him give the Prince of Wales a corned-beef-and-cabbage dinner in London, once. Wales liked it so much that he retaliated with a gift of four cases of champagne. And we like it. That's why we'll be seeing more of this young gentleman under two flags.

The stage hands who have been working with Fred on the set say he's the best crap-shooter north of Louisiana, too.

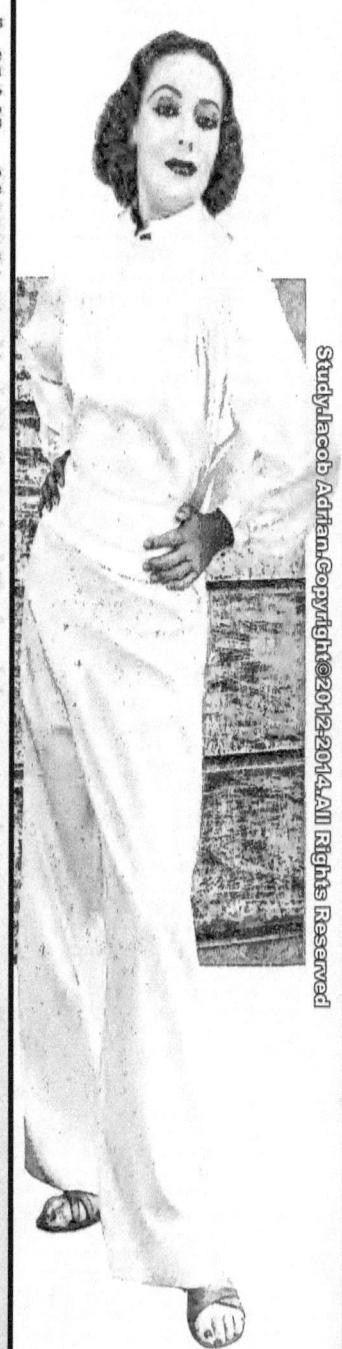

The glamorous Dolores Del Rio is one of the inner circle in Hollywood's exclusive society. Her comments on these pages take you with her on a round of social gayety

Bibliographic sources :

Hollywood (1934-1943)
Publisher: Hollywood Magazine, inc. ; Fawcett Publications, inc.

The New Movie Magazine (1929-1935)
Publisher: Tower Magazines, inc.

This documentary study use,
combined in various proportions,
elements from the following categories,
forms and subsets :
- fair use
- documentary
- documentary photography
- feature
- journalism
- arts journalism
- visual journalism
- photojournalism
- celebrity photography
in order to :
- employ material as the object of cultural critique ,
- quote to illustrate an argument or point ,
- use material in historical sequence,
providing independent opinion,
using photos, press articles, advertisements,
opinions of fans etc. ...

www.ingramcontent.com/pod-product-compliance
Lightning Source LLC
Chambersburg PA
CBHW021039180526
45163CB00005B/2190